THE ILLUSTRATED BIBLE FOR CHILDREN

THE ILLUSTRATED BIBLE FOR CHILDREN

Re-told by Ray Hughes

Illustrations by Nino Musio

Published in the United States and Canada by

Joshua Morris Publishing, Inc.
221 Danbury Road
Wilton, Connecticut 06897

Prepared by The Hamlyn Publishing Group Limited
Michelin House, 81 Fulham Road
London SW3 6RB, England

Fifth Printing 1992
Printed in Hong Kong
ISBN 0-88705-161-8

Contents

The Old Testament ——————————— 10

The New Testament ——————————— 157

Index of Stories
     and Bible references ——————— 268

Maps

    Palestine in the time of Our Lord ——————— 158

    The Missionary journeys of the apostle Paul ———— 256

In the beginning

Have you ever wondered how this marvellous world came to be? Who made all the stars, the earth, and the water in the sea? Who thought of making all the many animals, fishes and birds? Who made the brown earth in which our food grows, and the trees and their fruits? And who put man in this wonderful world and gave him eyes to see it? And who arranged the food for every insect, bird and fish?

At first, there was no earth, no sky, no trees, no people, or any animals. There was only a great mass of water and clouds, without any shape. All was black and empty, and nothing could be seen. Then God spoke. The first thing He said was, "Let light come." At once, light came, and God saw that it was good. The light was separated from darkness and God called the light day. He called the darkness night. That was the first day of all.

On the second day, God said, "Let there be a space between the waters." This space God called Heaven and underneath was nothing but water.

On the third day, God said, "Let the waters underneath be gathered together into oceans, so that dry land appears." And that is

what happened. God called the dry land earth, and the waters which were gathered together in the places He called seas. On that day God also said, "Let grass and plants and trees appear, with all kinds of fruit, and let them all have seeds so that more can grow." God saw it all and was pleased with His work.

On the fourth day, God said, "Let there be lights in the heavens to make days and nights and years." Then God made the great sun, to shine on the earth and bring warmth to its surface by day. He made the moon to give a soft light by night.

On the fifth day, God said, "Let all kinds of creatures come." The seas began to fill with colourful fish and creatures of all shapes and sizes. In the air, many kinds of birds, great and small, began to fly. On the land came creatures that crawled and crept, that ran and jumped, and climbed and burrowed into the earth.

God saw it all and He knew it was good.

On the sixth and last day that God worked, He made something else very wonderful. He said, "Let Us make someone like Ourselves, someone special who can think and understand and speak. Someone to look after the animals and all the plants. Let Us make someone with whom We can talk, someone different from all the other creatures." And this is what God did. From the dust of the ground He formed a man's body and then He breathed into him the breath of life. He called the man Adam.

Then God put the man to live in a lovely garden He had planted. Adam was told to look after it, and tend it. The Lord God also brought all the animals and birds to the man to see what he would call them. So Adam gave them all names.

Then God said, "It is not good for Adam to be by himself. I will make another person to be with him, to help him." So God caused a deep sleep to fall on Adam, and while he was asleep he removed one of Adam's ribs and made a beautiful woman from it. Then God brought the woman He had made to the man and Adam was so pleased and surprised, he exclaimed: "She is part of me, we are made for each other!" And Adam called the woman Eve. Adam and Eve were happy together.

And so God had finished making everything, from the heavens to the beautiful garden where the man and his wife were to live.

God looked at everything He had made, and there was nothing wrong with it. It was all very good.

On the seventh day God rested from all His work of creation.

In the beautiful garden

The garden where Adam and Eve lived was indeed very beautiful. There were pretty flowers and fine trees growing there full of all kinds of delicious fruits. Adam and Eve walked barefoot over grass, enjoying the sweet-smelling plants. There was nothing to hurt them in the garden. They were never cross, nor did they quarrel with each other, neither did they become ill or feel cold. Around them the animals romped and played, and the birds sang together. Every creature was completely happy. There were no harmful plants, no fierce beasts or biting insects. In the garden God planted also the tree of life and the tree of the knowledge of good and evil.

Rivers ran through this garden, and gold and precious stones were to be found there, too. In the evenings the Lord God came to talk with Adam and his wife.

"You may eat the fruits from any tree in the garden, except one," He said. "That one is called the tree of the knowledge of good and evil. You must not eat the fruit of that tree. For," God said, "on the day you eat the fruit of that tree you will surely die."

Die? Everything in the garden of Eden lived, there was nothing rotten or diseased, and every creature enjoyed a full, healthy and happy life. But, if Adam should take the fruit of that tree, it would not be like that any longer, and from the very day he ate it, trouble and death would come into the world.

So Adam and Eve enjoyed the garden and looked after it, and cared for all the animals.

At that time there was one creature God had made who was especially cunning and clever. It was the serpent. He came to Eve and talked with her. He talked about the trees in the garden. And then very craftily he asked, "Did God say you could eat from every tree in the garden?"

"Oh yes," answered Eve, "we may eat from every tree except the tree in the centre of the garden, the tree of the knowledge of good and evil. We may not eat fruit from that one. God said if we do, we will die."

"Oh no!" said the serpent. "You will not die; how can it be that God will not let you eat the fruit of that tree? It is because God knows that fruit would bring you understanding. It would make you wise, like God Himself, and you would know all about good and evil. God is trying to keep all that from you."

Eve believed all the serpent said, and she looked at the tree. It did look good. She thought she would really love to have some of that fruit. The more she looked, the more desirable it became. How fresh and lovely it was! Besides, she thought, how clever she would become!

"Go on!" urged the serpent. "Try it."

Should she? Why not? Trembling, she reached out and took the fruit and ate it. She gave some to her husband also, and he did just what God had forbidden him to do.

At once they felt different. They were ashamed of their bodies, and so they made clothes from fig leaves.

That evening they heard the sound of the Lord God walking in the garden. They tried to hide themselves away from Him, and from His presence.

"Where are you, Adam?" the Lord called.

Adam answered, "I heard you coming, I hid myself among the trees. I was afraid. I feel naked and ashamed now."

Then God demanded, "Why do you feel like that? What have you done? Have you eaten fruit from the tree I told you not to touch?"

Adam felt guilty. He had been found out. He knew that he had done wrong and had disobeyed the Lord's command. He tried to make an excuse, and blamed his wife.

"It was the woman You gave to be with me – she gave me the fruit of the tree, and I took it and ate it." Adam almost said, "It was Your fault, God. You gave her to me and she is to blame. She is the one who did it."

The Lord God turned to Eve. "What have you done?" He asked.

She also had an excuse. "It was the serpent. He deceived me," she said.

Then God spoke to the serpent. "You shall no longer be wise and bright and attractive. You will be changed and have to squirm on your belly. You have been used by Satan to bring about the downfall of the man I have made. You and yours will be enemies of My people, but in the end you will be crushed and defeated."

Then God spoke also to Eve. "When you have your babies it is going to be painful for you now, and your husband will be your master."

To Adam, God said, "Because you listened to your wife and disobeyed My command, you are going to have to work hard to get your food now. Thorns and thistles will come, and many troubles that you have not known before. After all your work, you will die and go back to the ground from which you came."

The Lord God made coats of animal skins for Adam and his wife to cover themselves. Then He drove them out of the beautiful garden of Eden. "They have now become like Us, they know good and evil, and now in case they also eat fruit from the tree of life and so live forever, they must leave the garden," said God.

He drove them out. So Adam had to dig and cultivate the earth to obtain his food. They were never to return to that lovely garden again.

At the east of the garden of Eden the Lord God placed cherubim, and a flaming sword, to guard the way to the tree of life, so that Adam and Eve could not reach fruit from that tree.

Cain and Abel

Life was not the same outside the lovely garden of Eden. The animals were not so friendly now, they growled and snarled and squawked. The land was bare. Plants and grass and trees did grow, but so did the thistles and the weeds. Adam and Eve were not nearly as happy and contented as they had been in Eden where everything had been so delightful. They sometimes quarrelled with each other, too; it had never been like that in the garden. Oh yes, there were many things that pleased them and which they enjoyed, but it was not the same as it had been there. Life was hard now. After working all day Adam was tired, and his body ached. Eve, too, had to work and help her husband. She made their clothes, and ground the wheat to make bread. Besides, she did not feel very well. She was going to have a baby.

Then Eve bore a child. It was the first baby that was ever born. They called the boy Cain, and he grew strong and helped his father in the fields.

Before long another baby arrived, and so Cain had a brother. They called him Abel. Later Adam and Eve had other boys and girls.

Abel liked animals, and when he grew up he looked after the sheep and cattle, so that there was wool to make clothes, and milk to drink. But Cain liked to grow things. He prepared the ground and grew grain, as well as all kinds of vegetables and fruit.

Now, Adam and Eve knew very well that they did not always do what was right. They did not please God all the time in the way they lived. Nor did their children. Ever since that day when they had disobeyed God in that lovely garden, things seemed to go wrong. They were sometimes irritable and the children argued and said things they should not say.

Then the time came when in order to obtain God's forgiveness for their disobedience, Cain and Abel offered Him gifts.

Cain preferred to worship in his own way, and chose to offer God some of the grain, vegetables and fruit he had grown. But Abel killed the best lamb he had, in the manner which he had been shown, and

offered that to God, asking Him to forgive him.

Abel's sacrifice was accepted by God, but that of Cain was rejected. Abel was thankful to God, and happy to know that he had been forgiven.

Now it made Cain angry that his brother's sacrifice should be accepted, and not his own.

The Lord spoke to Cain and asked him, "Why are you angry? If you would worship rightly you would be happy." Then God suggested to Cain, "There is a proper offering you could bring. If you do what is right, your sacrifice will be accepted as your brother's is accepted, and he will look up to you and respect you as his older brother and as the firstborn in the family."

But Cain did not worship as he had been taught. People who do not obey God become very unhappy. They begin to have bad feelings about God and about other people too. Cain felt bitter toward his brother Abel and picked a quarrel with him. He began to hate his brother and to have resentment in his heart toward Abel. One day Cain became so angry with him that he struck Abel a mighty blow, and so killed his brother. He lay on the ground, dead.

It is a great sin to take away another person's life in anger. If Cain's heart had been full of love for his brother, as it should have been, this would never have happened. It made Adam and Eve so sad to find the second person to be born to them in this world was dead.

Abel's God was grieved in His heart, also. He came to Cain and asked "Where is your brother Abel?" Cain answered back, "How do I know? Am I supposed to look after him?" God said, "What have you done? Because you have spilt your brother's blood, people will not accept you. Therefore you will wander for the rest of your life."

But even then, God was kind to Cain, and prevented anyone from killing him, although he had killed his brother.

The flood

Now Cain moved to another land, away from the presence of God. He married, and had very gifted and clever children and grandchildren. Cain's mother, Eve, was very sad and grieved that her son Abel had died, but God gave her another boy whom she called Seth. He and his children grew up to love the Lord God and to worship Him as Abel had done.

Adam and Eve had other sons and daughters, and lots of grandchildren, too. There were now many people alive on the earth and they lived to a great age in those days. But as time passed, and the first people who lived on earth died, men and women forgot their God, and what they had known about Him. They quarrelled, stole, and lied and cheated. They became evil and selfish.

The Lord looked on the earth and saw that the people had become bad and violent. It grieved Him in His heart so much that He was sorry that He had ever made man at all. He said:

"The people have become vile and cruel. I cannot have them living on My earth any longer. I will put an end to all this wickedness. All these people shall be destroyed."

How different it all was now. Once there had been love and harmony in all God's wonderful world; and now it was all spoiled. Hate, greed and fear, and all kinds of evil had come in. Men were unkind to one another and even children were being hurt.

There was one man, however, in whom God delighted. There was one man who loved and obeyed Him, and wanted to live to please the Lord his God. His name was Noah. He walked and talked with God. God spoke to Noah and told him what He was going to do.

"I am going to send a great flood of water over the whole earth," He said. "Now, Noah, this is what you must do. You are to build an ark, and you and your wife, and your three sons and their wives will go into it. I promise to save you from the great flood that is coming."

Noah believed what God had said, and began to build the ark as God had shown him. There were to be three floors, or decks, in the ark, and all around the top, under the roof, was to be a skylight, or window. A great door was to be built in the side. The ark was to be four hundred and fifty feet long, seventy-five feet wide, and forty-five feet high. This huge kind of boat would take Noah and his sons a long time to build.

So Noah began to build the ark as God commanded him. He and his sons set to work to cut down cypress trees, shape the timbers and fasten them together. Then they coated the ark with pitch, inside and outside, to keep out the water. It was hard work, and it took them many, many months to build the vessel. People came to see what Noah was building, and when they heard what it was, they laughed. "You are crazy, Noah. Fancy building a boat here!"

Then Noah told them what God said was going to happen, and why the great flood was coming – and they laughed all the more. They did not believe him.

At last the ark was finished, and Noah and his sons began to gather all kinds of stores to put in the ark, as God had told him. The neighbours watched as hay and vegetables, grain and fruit were stacked away inside.

Then God said, "Now all kinds of animals and birds will come into the ark. See that there are two of every sort, male and female, so that they may all be preserved, but take seven each of all the clean animals and birds. In seven days from now the rain will begin, and I will destroy every living creature that is not in the ark. It is going to rain without ceasing for forty days and forty nights."

So Noah and his family were busy for seven days getting all the creatures which God sent to him into their places in the ark. A tremendous number of animals of all kinds were assembled around the ark. Inside, Noah's sons were putting them all in the compartments which had been made for them. Lions and tigers, all kinds of monkeys, cats and dogs, bears and kangaroos. All creatures great and small. There were places for all the birds to roost and corners into which all the lizards and insects could crawl. At last it was done and all was ready. The animals all settled down to rest and sleep. God said to Noah and his family, "Now, you go into the ark, I have promised to save you alive."

So God made a covenant, or agreement, with Noah and He promised to look after him and his family. The door of the ark was shut, and it began to rain. It rained and rained, and rained. All day it rained, and all night, and the next day. It continued to rain without stopping for almost six whole weeks. Water welled up from under the earth also, and the ark began to float. It was lifted up, and rode on top of the waters. Inside, Noah's family of eight persons, and all the

animals and birds were safe. Outside, the water swirled about the hills and crept higher and higher until even the mountains were covered, and every creature was drowned. None escaped, except those who had come into the ark which Noah had built.

Then, at last, the rain stopped. Noah looked out of the window of the ark. There was water everywhere, even the mountain tops were covered. It took many days for the water to go down. Then Noah opened the window, and sent out a raven which kept flying around, but could find nowhere to perch. Next, he sent out a dove to see if she could find any dry land, but she returned. Another week passed, and he sent her out again. This time she returned with a fresh olive leaf which she had plucked. After another seven days he sent her out again. This time she did not come back to him.

Noah removed the covering of the ark and looked about him. It had come to rest on Mount Ararat, and Noah saw that the ground around him was now dry. The water had at last drained away from the surface of the earth.

Then God said to Noah, "Come out of the ark with your wife and your three sons and their wives. Bring out every living creature and all the birds, and make a fresh start. Let them all have their young and let them multiply and fill the earth again."

So Noah came out of the ark, and all the animals with him, and he took some of the clean beasts and birds, and built an altar and offered a burnt sacrifice to God. Noah worshipped the God of Heaven and gave thanks to Him.

How good it was to be on dry land once more. How thankful Noah was that he and his family and all the animals had been kept alive in the ark. They could now make a new start. The birds were released and flew in the air. The elephants came lumbering out. The donkeys trotted together. The other animals bounded away, and all the insects and other creatures crawled away to make new homes for themselves. "Never again will I send the waters to flood and destroy everything on the earth," said God. "Whenever you see the rainbow in the sky it is to remind you of this promise: that I will never again bring a flood like this on the earth to sweep away every living thing."

The tower of Babel

After the great flood, Noah's sons and their wives began to have children who grew up and had more children. Presently, there were again many families on the earth. As the people moved on towards the west, they came to the plain of Shinar.

"Ah!" they said, "this would be a grand place for us to settle down. We could make a fine city here and all live together." So they began to make many bricks for all the houses and buildings they wanted. Then they said to one another, "Why should we go any further? Let us stay here and be comfortable and let us make ourselves great. We do not want to be scattered all over the world. And let us build a huge tower – so tall that it would reach right up to the heavens."

Their hearts were full of pride and their own self-importance. They wanted to say, "Look what we have done!"

Now God had said that they were to go out into all the world, and fill it and look after it and develop it for Him. The Lord God was not pleased that the people did not want to do as He had commanded. So He came down to see the city.

"Now the people have begun to do wrong again," said God. "Because they have only one language, they stay together and will not spread over the earth."

So God caused them to speak in different languages. Next day, they could not work together easily because each could not understand the other. It was as if they were speaking nonsense.

At length, they formed themselves into groups by language, and left the city and its high tower. They began to go out and cultivate other parts of the world, as God had told them to do.

They called that city Babel, or Babylon. It was there that God caused them to "babble" in different languages, and in that way He made sure that the people spread out over the whole earth.

God calls Abram

The three sons of Noah were Shem, Ham and Japheth, and their families made their way to different parts of the world.

Now Abram lived about four hundred years after the flood, and he came from the family of Seth, whom God had blessed. Abram lived at Ur in Chaldea. Then there came a time when God appeared to him and made the great promise, saying:

"Leave the country in which you live, and your relations, and go to a land I will show you. I am going to make you into a great nation, Abram, and through you, and that nation, shall come blessing to all peoples of the world."

Abram leaves his home

So Abram moved out of Ur, as God had commanded him. He took with him Sarai, his wife, Terah, his father, and Lot, his nephew, and they came to Haran. They stopped at Haran, and there Terah died and was buried. Abram then moved on to the land of Canaan with all his servants and his cattle. It was a long, long journey, and it took them many months to reach Canaan.

When they rested there, God said to Abram, "This is the land I am giving to you and your descendants."

Then Abram built an altar on the spot where the Lord God appeared to him, and he worshipped the Lord. Afterwards, Abram travelled around the country to see the land God had given him. The Canaanites were still living there. Abram pitched his tent among the hills near to Bethel. From there, he moved his flocks of cattle and sheep to different places as they had need of pasture.

Abram and Lot

The servants of Lot, Abram's nephew, were always quarrelling with the servants of Abram over where their animals should feed. Lot had also become rich in herds of cattle. So Abram said to Lot, "Let there be no quarrelling between us. It is best if we separate and go different ways. Would you like to choose which way you want to go, and I will go the other way."

Lot looked around and he saw that the valley of the River Jordan was lush and green. This would be very good for his cattle. It looked beautiful, and fertile.

"I will have all the plain of Jordan," he said. And so they parted.

Lot went to live among the cities of the plain and he pitched his tent near Sodom. But the men of Sodom were evil before God.

As soon as Lot had gone, God said to Abram again, "All the land you see is yours. I am giving it to you and your children. There is going to be a great nation of people coming from you." It was as if God said, "Abram, you have let Lot have the best part of the land – but really it is all yours. It is the land I am giving you."

However, Lot was soon in danger. Some tribes who lived in the hills decided to invade the cities of the plain. They came and fought with the people who lived there. They defeated the cities of Sodom and Gomorrah, and took away all they could from those cities. They also captured Lot and all he had.

But one person escaped and came and told Abram that Lot and all his people had been taken away captive. Abram armed all his men and marched off in the night after the raiders. He had 318 trusty servants. They caught up with the invaders and defeated them. Abram rescued his nephew Lot, his family and servants, and all their goods, and brought them back again.

On the way back, God's priest met Abram and blessed him. Once more, God spoke to Abram and promised to reward him. Then Abram said to God, "But, Lord, I have no children of my own. My wife and I are growing too old to have a child now. How can Your promise come true?"

God's promise

God replied: "You will have a son, and your family will become a great nation. There will be more people than you can count. Now look up at the starry sky and begin to count the stars on a clear night; you will never finish counting them, there are so many. Your family, all your descendants, will be more than the number of stars in the heavens."

Abram believed God, even when he could not understand how it could happen. He worshipped the Lord God with a sacrifice and God told him more about what was going to happen to his family.

"Abram, your descendants are going to be slaves in another land for four hundred years. They are going to suffer. But at the end of that time, I will punish the nation that made them slaves, and they will come away with wealth and many possessions."

Now, Sarai his wife had a maidservant whom she had brought back from Egypt. Her name was Hagar. Sarai agreed that Hagar should have a son for Abram, and so Ishmael was born. But it caused trouble in the family. This was not the son God had promised.

"No," said the Lord to Abram. "Sarai, your wife, shall have a son herself, and his name is to be Isaac. I am changing your wife's name from Sarai to Sarah, which means 'princess', and I am changing your name from Abram to Abraham, 'the father of many'."

God made a solemn promise to Abraham. "When he is born, Isaac is to be the one through whom I will bless the whole world."

But still no baby came.

Then one day, Abraham was sitting at his tent door in the heat of the day when he saw three men. There was something special about them. They did not look quite like ordinary men.

"Do not pass by," Abraham said to them. "Come and wash and refresh yourselves. Stop and I will get you something to eat."

He called to Sarah, "Prepare a meal for these men; some fresh bread, tender meat, and milk for them to drink."

So they agreed to stop and talk to Abraham. "Where is your wife, Sarah?" they asked. "She is in the tent," answered Abraham. Then they gave him some good news.

"This time next year Sarah is going to have a son," they told him.

Now Sarah was listening behind the tent door, and she laughed. "I am too old to have a baby now," she said to herself.

Then the Lord said to Abraham: "Why did Sarah laugh, and say, 'Am I really going to have a baby?'" Then, He said, "Is there anything which the Lord cannot do? I promise you Sarah will have a son by this time next year."

The men got up to go. They turned toward Sodom. Abraham liked talking with them, and they walked along the road together. The Lord said, "Shall I tell Abraham what I am going to do? I have chosen him. I know that he will bring up his children to keep my way and do that which is right and just. No, I will not hide from Abraham what is going to happen."

"Abraham," God said, "the sins of the people of Sodom and Gomorrah are very grievous. I am going down there now."

Abraham was alarmed. His relative Lot was there. Lot had in fact moved into the city of Sodom itself. Abraham prayed to the Lord.

"Suppose there are godly people there – will You really destroy those people with all the wicked ones? If there are fifty of Your people there, You would not sweep away the righteous ones with the wicked, would You? Surely, the Judge of the earth will do right?"

The Lord answered Abraham, "If I find fifty righteous people in Sodom I will not destroy the city."

Abraham spoke again. "May I speak again? I ought to be careful how I speak to You, O God. But, suppose there are only forty-five righteous people there? Will You still destroy the whole city?"

"If I find forty-five righteous people there, I will not destroy the city," God responded.

"Suppose there are only forty?" Abraham asked.

"I will not do it if there are forty," said the Lord.

"Do not be angry with me," pleaded Abraham. "Will You – if there are only thirty?"

"I will not do it if there are thirty," the Lord replied.

"Twenty?" asked Abraham.

"Not for twenty," the Lord replied.

"May I speak this last time?" Abraham asked. "What if only ten righteous can be found there?"

God answered, "For the sake of ten, I will not destroy the city."

Then the Lord left him, and Abraham went back home to his tent.

Lot escapes

The two angels went down to Sodom, arriving in the evening. They met Lot who bowed down to them and asked them to stay at his house that night. They said that they would not trouble him, but he urged them to wash and eat and rest at his home.

That night the wicked men of Sodom came to Lot's house and demanded that he send the men out so that they could attack them. The men of Sodom began to get violent, but they were struck with blindness and could not find the door of Lot's house to break down.

The two men said to Lot, "Take your family out of here quickly. God is going to destroy this whole city. Hurry!"

The husbands of Lot's daughters did not believe Lot. They thought he was joking. The two heavenly messengers said to Lot at daybreak, "You must go, or you will all be destroyed in this city!"

Lot, his wife, and his daughters, still lingered. The angels took them by the hand and hurried them away. "Escape for your life, don't stop anywhere in the plain! And don't look back until you get to the mountains! Nothing can be done until you are out!"

As soon as Lot, his wife, and his daughters were away the Lord rained down fire and burning sulphur out of the heavens and destroyed all those wicked cities of the plain.

Abraham got up that morning and looked down toward Sodom and Gomorrah and he saw the smoke of the burned out cities. But God had remembered the prayer of Abraham and saved Lot out of that burning fiery destruction.

Isaac is born

God also remembered His promise to Abraham and Sarah. The baby came for which they had waited so long. How happy they were when little Isaac was born!

He grew up a strong lad and was able to help his father with all the cattle and the sheep.

Where is the lamb?

Again God spoke to Abraham. But it was different this time.

"Abraham!" God called.

"Yes, Lord, I'm here," Abraham replied.

Then God said a very strange thing.

"I want you to go with your son, Isaac, your only son whom you love very dearly, to the land of Moriah, and to one of the mountains which I shall show you. I want you to sacrifice him there as a burnt offering."

Abraham could not understand this. He had waited so long for his son. God had given him Isaac as He had promised, and now, now the Lord God was asking for him to be sacrificed. How was God going to make from Abraham's son the family, the tribe, the nation He had promised, if Isaac was to be offered as a sacrifice to God? What a fine, strong lad he was, and now he was to die. Abraham could not understand. Why did it have to be?

But even as Abraham had always obeyed God, so he did now. Early next morning he arose and prepared for the journey. It would take them three days. He saddled his donkey and gathered together all they would need. He cut the wood for the burnt offering and took some food and water. With two servants, Abraham and Isaac set off.

On the third day of their journey, Abraham looked up and saw the place where he was to go. He stopped, and said to his two servants, "You stay here with the donkey. My boy and I are going up the mountain to the place where we have to worship, and then we will come back again to you."

Abraham put the wood on his son's shoulder, and carrying the knife and the fire himself, he and the boy began to climb the mountain together. As they were going, Isaac said, "My father."

"Yes, my son?" answered Abraham.

"We have the fire and the wood, but where is the lamb for the burnt offering?"

"God will provide Himself a lamb," Abraham said.

At last the boy and his father reached the place of sacrifice, and Abraham slowly gathered stones with his son to build the altar. When it was built, he explained to Isaac what the Lord had told him to do. Abraham arranged the wood in place, after which Isaac was laid on the altar and was bound there with cords. Then Abraham went to pick up the knife to slay his son. A voice from Heaven rang out:

"Abraham! Abraham!"

Abraham was startled. "I am here, Lord, I am here."

"Do not lay your hands on the lad. Do nothing to hurt him, for now I know that you reverence God, since you have not even kept your son, your only son, from Me."

Abraham untied the cords that bound his son. And as he looked, there behind him was a ram caught in a thicket by its horns. So Abraham took the ram and offered it up for a burnt offering, instead of his son.

Abraham called that mountain 'The Lord will provide', because the Lord did provide a sacrifice for Himself. Once more, God reminded Abraham of His promises, and blessed him there.

So Abraham and Isaac went back to the men, and they returned home, where Abraham taught Isaac all he knew. He trained his son to love God and to live to please Him in every way.

The twins

Sarah, Isaac's mother, lived to be 127 years old. When she died, Abraham was very sad, and buried her in a cave near Hebron.

Abraham called his chief servant. "It is time my son was married. He is not to marry any of the Canaanite women, for the Canaanites do not love or serve the Lord. I want you to go back to the country from which I came, to my native land where I was born, and find a wife for my son from among the people there. Isaac is not to go back there because this land is the land which God has given us, and this is where we are to live. Promise me that you will do this. God will send His angel, and will guide you to the right girl for my son."

When, after many days, the servant arrived back in the land of Mesopotamia from which Abraham had come, he reached the city of Nahor. There, outside the city, he made the camels kneel down by a well of water. It was evening and the women came to draw water out of the well. Abraham's servant prayed, "O Lord God of my master Abraham, help me to know which one of the women of this city is the chosen one. When I say, 'Please may I have a drink out of your jar of water', and she says, 'You can have a drink, and I will give your camels some water as well', I shall know that this is the one whom you have chosen for Isaac."

As the servant finished speaking to the Lord God, a girl with a pitcher on her shoulder came to the well. She was very beautiful. She went down to fill the jar full of water from the well, and as she came back, Abraham's servant ran to meet her. "Please let me drink a little water from your pitcher," he asked.

"Drink," she said, letting her pitcher down for him to quench his thirst, and then she said, "I will give your camels water as well," and, emptying her pitcher into the trough, she ran back to the well.

The servant watched her, wondering. Then he brought out a golden ring, and put two gold bracelets on her wrists.

"Whose daughter are you?" he asked, "and please tell me, is there room in your father's house for me to spend the night?"

The girl told him who she was, and said, "Yes, we have plenty of

straw and food for your camels, and there is room for you to stay the night."

Then Abraham's servant bowed his head, and worshipped the Lord for helping him to find the right house. For it was the house of members of his master's family. Rebekah was the girl's name.

Rebekah ran home to tell her family. When her brother Laban saw her ring and the golden bracelets, and heard about the man, he went out and invited Abraham's servant into the house. The servant told the family much concerning his master, and how God had blessed him, then he gave them the presents he had brought. He told them how God had led him to find Rebekah, and that she was the chosen one to be Abraham's son's wife. Laban agreed that she should go, because it was the Lord's command, and so Rebekah too agreed to go back with him and become Isaac's wife. Her maids travelled with her. When at last they arrived at Isaac's home, he greeted her joyfully and soon she became his wife. She was very beautiful, and he loved her.

The years went by, and they had no children, but Isaac prayed to the Lord, and the Lord answered his prayers. The day came when God told Rebekah at last that she would have twin children.

Now, the firstborn usually has first place in the family. But God told Rebekah that of her children, it would be the one who came second who would be the one to inherit the family blessing.

At length the twins were born. The first boy was called Esau, and the second, Jacob.

As the boys grew they became very different. Esau became a skilful hunter, and loved to be out in the hills. But Jacob was a quiet man who preferred to work around the home. Isaac loved Esau, but Rebekah was more fond of Jacob.

One day, Jacob was cooking a meal. It was a red stew. Esau came in from the fields, and he was very tired and hungry.

"Please let me have some of your stew, for I am faint from hunger," Esau pleaded with Jacob.

"I will give you some stew," Jacob replied, "but only if you will sell me your birthright." By that he meant that, in exchange for the food, he would take all the privileges and rights in the family which Esau had as firstborn.

"I must have that stew, or I shall surely die," Esau replied.

"Make a solemn promise to me that your birthright is mine," Jacob demanded.

So Esau sold his birthright to his brother Jacob for a bowl of stew. The food was more important to him then than his birthright.

But Esau did not respect God's laws and he married heathen wives who did not love and believe in the Lord. That made Isaac and Rebekah very unhappy.

Isaac was growing very old and he could no longer see. He thought it was time to give his older son the family blessing as the custom was. He called Esau.

"Yes, my father," Esau responded.

"The time for me to die is drawing nearer. As my firstborn son, I want to give you my blessing before I go. Take your bow and your arrows, and go out into the country and hunt game for me. Bring it back and make me the savoury meat that I love, and I will give you my blessing."

Now Rebekah, Isaac's wife, overheard him speaking to Esau, and as soon as he had gone out to hunt, she called Jacob. She told him what Isaac had said to his brother.

"Now, my son, listen to me. Go out to our flock and bring me two choice young goats and I will prepare food as your father loves it. Then you take it in to him, and he will give his blessing to you."

Jacob did all his mother told him to do. Then he went to his father.

"I am here, my father," said Jacob.

"Who is that?" asked Isaac.

"It is Esau, your firstborn son," Jacob lied. "I have made you the savoury meat that you love."

"Are you really my son Esau?"

"I am," Jacob replied.

"Then I will eat your meal."

When Isaac was satisfied he said, "Come here, my son." And he blessed Jacob with a great blessing. Jacob and his children after him were to be the ones to have the family blessing of God, for ever.

As soon as Isaac had ended the blessing of his son, and Jacob had departed, Esau came in with the deer that he had killed. He set to work to prepare it, and cook it, and then brought it in to his father.

"Come, father, eat my food so that you may bless me," Esau said.

"Who are you?" asked Isaac in astonishment.

"I am Esau, your eldest son," he replied.

Isaac trembled. "Then who was it who brought me that meal I have just eaten? I blessed him – and he is now blessed."

Esau gave a loud and bitter wail. "Bless me as well!" he cried.

"Your brother has had your blessing," replied Isaac. "What can I do for you now?" And so he gave Esau a different blessing.

"When my father is dead," swore Esau, "I will kill my brother!"

When Rebekah heard that Esau had said this, she spoke to Isaac. "It is time Jacob was married," she said. "He ought not to marry one of the heathen women in this country who do not worship the Lord our God.''

Then Isaac called for Jacob. ''I do not want you to marry one of the women of Canaan. I want you to go to the land from which your mother came, and find yourself a wife there.'' And Isaac blessed Jacob again. ''You and your family will inherit this land which God gave to Abraham,'' he said.

Then Rebekah spoke to Jacob. ''Your brother intends to kill you as soon as your father is dead. Go to my brother Laban's house in Haran and stay there a while until Esau has forgotten his anger against you.''

So Jacob left home for the long journey to Haran. That night he rested his head on a stone for a pillow. He dreamed, and in his dream he saw steps reaching from earth to Heaven, and going up and down the steps he saw angels.

Then, God spoke to him. He said: ''I am the Lord your God. I am giving you this land, Jacob. It is for you and all your descendants. I am going to be with you and look after you, that I promise. All the peoples of the earth will be blessed through your family.''

In the morning, Jacob arose. He exclaimed, ''God is in this place, and I did not know it! I knew that He was with my father, but He is also with me, here!''

Then he took the stone he had used for a pillow, and set it up. He poured some oil on to it and he said: ''This is going to be a special place. I will call it Bethel.'' (This means 'the house of God'.) ''If God is going to look after me and keep me, and bring me back to this land again, this stone will mark the place of God's house. And of all that You give me, God, I will give You back a tenth of it.''

For many days Jacob walked on toward Haran. At last he came to a well where the flocks of sheep were brought to drink.

''Where do you people come from?'' Jacob asked.

''From Haran,'' was the reply.

''Do you know Laban?'' Jacob asked next.

''Yes, we know him,'' they said.

''Is he well?''

''Yes, he is well – and look, that is his daughter Rachel bringing his sheep to drink at the well.''

When Jacob saw her coming he was so pleased to meet her. He rolled the heavy stone back so that she did not have to wait. Then he told Rachel that he was Rebekah's son, and kin to her. When Rachel returned home she told her father about Jacob, and Laban ran out to meet Jacob and hear the news of his family.

So Jacob stayed with them. After a while, Laban said, ''Would you

like to stay here and work for me? And why should you not be paid? Tell me what your wages should be."

Now Laban had two daughters, Leah and Rachel. But Jacob loved Rachel. "I will work on your farm for seven years if you will let me marry Rachel," he said.

So Jacob worked for Laban for seven years, but it seemed like only a few days, because of the love he had for Laban's daughter Rachel.

But when the wedding day came, Laban gave Jacob his daughter Leah. Jacob was angry. He said, "I have worked seven years because you promised I should wed Rachel. Why have you done this? You have cheated me."

Laban said, "It is the rule in our country to give the firstborn to be married first. But you may marry Rachel also, if you promise to work for me for another seven years."

Then Jacob had to work another seven years for Rachel, whom he loved.

Children began to be born to Jacob, and soon he had a large family.

Then at last Jacob said to Laban, "I have served you well, but now I would like to go back to my own country."

But Laban said, "We have done well together; my farm was quite small before you came. Since you came it has grown very prosperous. Please stay. Tell me what you want for wages, and I will pay you."

"I need cattle of my own," said Jacob. "You give me all the cattle born speckled, or spotted, and you can have all the rest."

Now Jacob knew how to breed cattle that were speckled and spotted, and he began to acquire a lot of cattle for himself. So Laban changed their agreement. But Jacob always knew a way to get more cattle for himself, and then Laban would alter the arrangement again.

At last, Jacob said, "I will not stay any longer." So, while Laban was away he gathered up all his family and his flocks and his herds and started out for his own country. The journey took a long time. The nearer he got to Canaan, the more worried he was at the thought of meeting his brother Esau whom he had wronged.

The night before they were to meet, God talked with Jacob and had a great struggle with him. Then, God changed Jacob's name to Israel.

The next day, Esau first saw all Jacob's family, and his flocks and herds. Then, last of all, came Jacob. The brothers met, but there was no anger between them. They wept and embraced, and Esau welcomed Jacob and his family. Then after a time they parted, and went to live in different parts of the country.

Joseph is sold

Jacob had twelve sons and a daughter. They pitched their tents at Bethel where God had spoken to him when he had left home to escape from Esau's anger.

Jacob said to his family: "Now you must destroy all those idols you have brought with you. You must worship the Lord God." So he built an altar there at Bethel and worshipped.

God blessed him, saying, "I gave this land to Abraham and to your father Isaac, and now I am giving it to you and your descendants."

Jacob's favourite sons were Joseph, and Benjamin who was the youngest. When Joseph was seventeen years old Jacob gave him a lovely coloured coat. He had never given his other sons anything like that. They were jealous of Joseph and began to hate him because he was his father's favourite.

One day Joseph said to his brothers, "I had a dream last night, and you were all in my dream. We were binding sheaves of corn. My sheaf stood upright, but all your sheaves stood round and bowed their heads down toward my sheaf."

But Joseph's description of the dream made his brothers hate him more than ever. "Do you think that we are all going to bow down to you one day?" they asked.

Then Joseph had another dream which he told to his father as well. "Listen to my dream," he said. "I saw the sun and the moon and eleven stars, and they all gathered around my star. What do you think that means?"

Joseph's father was not pleased to hear about that dream, either. "Do you think that your mother and father, as well as your brothers, are actually going to bow down to you?" he asked.

The brothers, except Joseph, had taken the flocks to find new grazing land for them. Some days later, Jacob said to Joseph, "Go and see if all is well." After some time, Joseph found them, but they saw him coming.

"Here comes that dreamer," they said. "What shall we do to him? Let's get rid of him. Let's kill him! We can tell his father that some

wild animal has eaten him. Then we'll see what happens to his dreams!"

But Reuben, the oldest brother, spoke up, "Let us not shed his blood. Why don't we just throw him in this pit, and leave him there?" Reuben thought that he would come back later and save the lad.

So, when Joseph came to them, his brothers took hold of him, pulled off his colourful coat, and threw him into the pit.

But Reuben went away while the other brothers sat down to eat their meal. As they were eating, they saw some Ishmaelites coming, their camels laden with spices to sell in Egypt. Then the brothers had another idea. "Let us sell Joseph to the Ishmaelites. We don't want to kill him, do we? After all, he is our brother." So, they pulled Joseph out of the pit and sold him to the traders for twenty pieces of silver.

Later, when Reuben came back and looked into the pit, Joseph was gone! "What shall I do?" he cried. "What shall I tell my father?"

The brothers told him what they had done. Then they killed a goat, and dipped Joseph's beautiful coat into the blood, and took it home to their father. "We found this," they said. "Is it your son's coat?"

Jacob tore his garments in anguish. "Some wild animal has devoured him. He has been torn to pieces!" Jacob cried, and he wept and mourned for his son for many days. All his family tried to comfort him, but he said, "I will mourn for my son Joseph every day until I die."

But what was happening to Joseph? In Egypt he was sold as a slave to Potiphar, who was captain of the king's bodyguard. Joseph became Potiphar's slave and worked in his house and on his land. He did his work well, and God was with him. Soon Potiphar found that Joseph was a reliable worker and could be trusted. He began to give him more and more to look after, until Joseph was put in charge of all Potiphar's affairs. "Since you have come, my house has been a very happy one, and all has gone well," Potiphar told Joseph.

Now, Potiphar's wife saw that Joseph was young and attractive. She wanted him to make love to her. But he said, "No, my master has wholeheartedly placed his trust in me with everything. I cannot betray him." She kept on asking him, but Joseph would have nothing to do with her.

One day, she pulled his coat off him, and called out to the other servants. "This man tried to molest me!" she told them. When her husband came home she told him the same story. "Why did you bring this wicked Hebrew slave here?" she demanded.

Potiphar believed what she said, and his anger burned against Joseph. He sent him straight to prison, although he had done no wrong.

But the Lord was with Joseph in prison, too. Joseph behaved himself and worked so well that the jailer put him in charge of all the other prisoners. Whatever Joseph did, and wherever Joseph was, God blessed him.

One day, the king of Egypt became angry with his head baker and chief butler, and threw them both into the prison.

They both had a dream one night. In the morning, when Joseph saw them he said, "What has happened to you? Why are you looking so glum this morning?" They answered, "We have both had a dream and we cannot tell the meaning."

"Everything has a meaning," Joseph told them, "and the Lord God knows the meaning. Tell me your dreams."

So the chief butler, whose job was to look after the king and all his drinks, began his story. "In my dream, I saw a grape vine in front of me. It had three branches. It was full of lovely clusters of ripe grapes. Pharaoh's cup was in my hand. I took the grapes and squeezed the juice into Pharaoh's cup, and gave it to him. What does it mean?"

"This is what it means," Joseph replied. "The three branches mean three days. Three days from now Pharaoh will release you from this prison and you will be serving the king his drinks again."

The chief baker was cheered when he heard the meaning of the chief butler's dream, so he told his dream to Joseph.

"In my dream, I had three baskets of bread and cakes on my head for Pharaoh. Then the birds came and began to eat out of my basket. What does this mean?"

"It means," answered Joseph, "that in three days Pharaoh will take you out of prison. You will be hanged, and the birds will come and eat your flesh."

It happened exactly as Joseph said. Before the butler was released from the prison, Joseph asked him if he would do him a kindness. "I was taken away from my home and sold here as a slave. I have done nothing wrong to cause me to be locked in here. Will you speak to Pharaoh and ask him to get me out of this place, please?"

But the butler forgot all about Joseph when he returned to Pharaoh's palace.

Pharaoh's dreams

Two more years passed by, and Joseph was still in the prison. No friends visited him, and there he had to stay.

One night, Pharaoh, King of Egypt, had a dream. It was very real to him. In his dream, he was standing on the brink of the river Nile, and he saw seven beautiful cows come up out of the river. They looked so fat and healthy. After them, came seven skinny and scrawny cows. The thin ugly cows then ate up the lovely plump ones. Pharaoh awoke and was troubled. Afterwards, he fell asleep again and had another dream. Now he saw growing seven ripe ears of corn, looking healthy and good. Seven more ears of corn appeared, all shrivelled up by the hot east wind. These seven bad ears swallowed up the good healthy ears of corn.

In the morning, when he woke up, he wondered whatever these two dreams could mean. Surely they meant something? He called for all his wise men and magicians to come to him, and he told them his dreams.

"What do they mean?" Pharaoh wanted to know.

They listened to the king. They looked at one another. But they could not think of any meaning of these dreams. Pharaoh's chief butler was there, and suddenly he remembered something.

"Oh King," he said, "I should have told you before this. When I was in prison with your head baker, we both had a dream the same night. We were worried, and a young Hebrew fellow in the prison explained to us the meaning of our dreams. He told your head baker that in three days he would be executed – and he was! He told me that in three days I would be released and have my job as chief butler back again. It happened exactly as he said."

"Where is this young man, and what is his name?" Pharaoh demanded. Joseph quickly changed out of his prison clothes, washed and shaved himself, and came before Pharaoh.

"None of my wise men can tell me the meaning of the dreams I had last night," said Pharaoh, "but I have heard that you can truly tell their meaning."

"Not I," said Joseph. "God will give Pharaoh the meaning of his dreams."

So Pharaoh described the two dreams to Joseph. The seven plump cows he had seen, and what happened to them; and the seven good ears of corn, and what happened to them.

Then Joseph answered. "The two dreams are about the same thing, and what is going to happen. God is showing Pharaoh what He is going to do. The seven good cows and the seven good ears of corn represent seven years. There will be seven very good years of harvest, and there will be plenty for both cattle and men to eat. But, in the next seven years after this period of plenty, there is going to be a drought and a terrible famine, and there will be no food for the people. Men and animals will starve. God gave the dream twice to Pharaoh so that you will know that this is certainly what will happen.

"Now," Joseph continued to the King, "let Pharaoh choose a wise man to arrange the construction of great buildings in which to save the grain, so that food may be stored up during those good harvest times which are coming. Then, you will have food for the people when the famine comes and they will not die. Let Pharaoh appoint men throughout the land to see that the grain is saved and not wasted during the next seven good years. That is what Pharaoh should do."

Pharaoh then talked with his officers. "Can we find anyone better than this man to look after all this for us?" he enquired. Turning to Joseph, he said:

"Because God Himself has shown you all this, I will put you in charge. Whatever you say is to be done, shall be done. I am giving you authority over all the land of Egypt. No one except myself shall be greater than you."

Pharaoh took off the splendid ring from his own finger and put it on Joseph's hand to show the honour he had given him. He also gave him fine clothes to wear, and then he put a gold chain around his neck.

So Pharaoh made Joseph his chief Minister of State, and also put him in charge of his palace. Joseph came from prison to be first minister in one day. He rode in Pharaoh's chariot as second-in-command, and travelled throughout the land to organize the work of building granaries and storing the harvest.

Soon it all began to happen as Joseph had said. There were seven years of bumper harvests and the grain siloes overflowed.

Joseph was not thirty years old. He married, and two boys were born to him.

The seven years of plenty came to an end and the seven years of famine began. In all the countries around the crops failed, and the people began to grow hungry. But in Egypt there was plenty of food. People from other lands heard that there was plenty of grain in Egypt, and they came to see if they could buy some. Pharaoh sent them to Joseph. He opened up the granaries, and he sold them the grain he had carefully stored away.

Joseph's brothers

Meanwhile, in the land of Canaan Joseph's family was running out of food, for there had been no rain and nothing would grow. When Joseph's father heard that there was corn in Egypt, he said to his sons, "Why don't you go down to Egypt? I hear that they have plenty of grain to sell there. If you do not go and buy some, we shall all starve to death!"

Jacob's ten sons therefore saddled their mules and made their way to Egypt. Benjamin, the youngest, they left behind, for he was his father's favourite son, now that Joseph had gone, and his father did not want anything to happen to him.

When they arrived in Egypt they found many people from other lands who wanted to buy corn as well. As Joseph was the governor of all the land and in charge of the sale of grain, the brothers were sent to him.

The last time the brothers had seen him he was only a lad of seventeen. Now, he was dressed differently from them; his face was shaved, and his hair was arranged in the Egyptian way. Around his neck was Pharaoh's great gold chain. Servants waited on him. Men weighed out the grain, others collected the money and kept a record of what was sold.

It came to the turn of these ten shepherd men from the hills of the land of Canaan to ask Joseph for food for their families. They looked at him with great respect and bowed down in front of him, without thinking for one minute who he might be! But Joseph recognized them, and he remembered his dreams of long ago. They were his own brothers. The dreams had come true. Here they were bowing down before him, just as it had been in his dreams.

Joseph wanted to tell them who he was, and to ask about his family and the young brother who was not with them. What sort of men were they now? Did they have hard thoughts in their hearts, as they had when he had last seen them?

He scowled at them.

"Where do you men come from?" he demanded. "You are spies

and have come to spy out the land. What are you doing here?"

"We are not spies," they protested. "We are all brothers from one family. We come from Canaan, and are honest men. Our father had twelve sons, one is dead and the other is at home. We have come only to buy food for our families. They are hungry."

Joseph was very happy to hear that his young brother Benjamin was alive and at home, but he still spoke sternly to the brothers.

"How do I know that? You are spies! Suppose you prove that you are true men. You will not leave Egypt until I see your other brother. One of you will go and get him and bring him here. Then, I shall know whether you have a younger brother, or not." With that, he put them all into prison for three days.

After three days Joseph saw them again. "As I am a man who respects God," he said, "I will let you go this time and take the food to your starving families, but one of you will stay here in prison until you bring back your youngest brother. Then, I shall know that you speak the truth. If you do not bring him, the brother you are leaving here will die."

Then, they talked among themselves in their own language.

"This has all come about because of what we did to young Joseph. We took no notice of his cries of distress. Now look what is happening to us!"

They could not forget that day.

"I told you not to sin against the boy," said Reuben.

They did not know that Joseph understood all they said as they were talking about him. They thought he was an Egyptian, for he had spoken to them through the man who was his interpreter.

Joseph wept as they talked. He turned and left the room so they could not see the tears in his eyes.

Then returning to them again, he chose Simeon, and had him bound. The brothers paid their money and waited while their sacks were filled with corn. Joseph had secretly instructed his men to put their money back in the top of their sacks, and to put in some food for their journey.

They loaded up their mules and were glad to be on their way home.

"Don't come back without your young brother Benjamin," Joseph warned them.

Joseph had frightened his brothers, but he had found out what he wanted to know. They were sorry for what they had done, and his father and young brother were alive and well.

When the brothers stopped to rest for the night, one of them opened his sack to feed the animals. He was astonished to see his money was in the top of his sack! Now they were really afraid. When they went back the man would say that they had not paid for their corn, and they would be in worse trouble. "Now we are being punished for what we did to our brother," they said to one another.

Arriving home, they told father Jacob all that had happened. "The lord of the land spoke very angrily to us," they said. "Simeon has had to stay in prison. He will not be released, and we can get no more food unless we take Benjamin with us. The man accused us of being spies. We told him that we were honest men, and not spies. We said that we were twelve sons of our father, one was at home, and one was dead, but he did not believe us. 'If you bring your young brother I will know that you are not spies but honest men. Then you may trade in the land and I will release to you this your brother,' he said."

"He shall not go," Jacob declared. "I have lost one of my young sons, I am not going to lose another!"

There was still no rain, and nothing would grow. Soon they were running out of the grain they had brought from Egypt. Jacob said to his sons, "We need some more food. Why don't you go back again to Egypt and get some for us?"

"We have to take Benjamin with us this time, otherwise, the man will kill us as spies," they reminded their father.

"Take him presents. Take double money this time," Jacob rejoined.

"We have to take our brother," the sons insisted.

"Why did you tell him that you had a young brother?" Jacob wanted to know.

They said, "The man asked questions about our family, about our father, and whether we had another brother. We did not know that he was going to say, 'Bring him down to Egypt'."

"I am losing all my children," cried Jacob. "Joseph is no more, Simeon is gone, and now you want to take young Benjamin away; everything is against me. He shall not go down to Egypt with you. His brother is dead and if anything should happen to him, that would be the end of me."

Then Judah said, "Father, I will look after him, I will keep him by me all the time. I promise to bring him back safe and sound. If we stay much longer we shall all die for lack of food! We cannot go down without Benjamin. The man said, 'Don't ever come back again unless you bring your brother.' If you do not send him, we shall not go, but if you do send him we shall be able to get grain, and our little ones will live. Otherwise, we shall all die of hunger. Send the boy with me; if I do not bring him back I will bear the blame before you all my life."

At last Jacob agreed to let Benjamin go. "Take some of our best things as presents for the man and take double the money with you. Look after my son Benjamin, and may God Almighty make the man kindly toward you! If my sons must die, they must die." So they took Benjamin, and arrived in Egypt.

Joseph had been waiting to see them, and when they came before him again, and he saw Benjamin was with them, he directed his servant to take them to his own home, saying, "Prepare a banquet for them and I will come and eat with them."

The brothers were afraid, and they wondered what was to become of them. "It is because of the money we found in our sacks," they said. So they spoke to the steward and explained how they had found their money bags.

"Oh Sir," they said, "on our way home we found our money in the top of our sacks, but now we have brought it back to you."

"Do not be afraid," the steward said, "I had your money."

Their mules were taken to be fed, and the men had a wash and prepared themselves to eat with the lord of the land. Simeon was released and joined his brothers.

When Joseph arrived home, they bowed down before him and offered him the presents they had brought.

"How is your father?" he asked, "and is this your younger brother of whom you told me? God be gracious to you, my son," he said to Benjamin.

Then the brothers bowed down before him again. Joseph was so glad to see his brothers, but especially Benjamin. A lump came up in his throat. He could not speak, and was about to cry. Quickly he left the room, dried his eyes, and washed his face, and came back again.

"Serve the meal," he ordered.

When they sat down they were all astonished, because they found that their places had been arranged according to their ages. How could the man do that? The servants brought the brothers their food from Joseph's table. Benjamin's share was larger than all the others. The brothers could not understand it, but they enjoyed their meal. They had not eaten such splendid food for a long time.

After they had eaten, Joseph commanded, "Fill the men's sacks with food and let them go."

Then he called his steward and told him secretly to put his own silver cup in Benjamin's sack.

Next morning, as soon as it was light, all the brothers loaded their mules and were off back to their homes again.

But before they had gone very far Joseph's steward came riding up after them.

"Stop!" he cried. "You have stolen my master's silver drinking cup. Why have you done this after all his kindness to you?"

"Why should your servants do a thing like that?" they exclaimed. "We would not do that. Didn't we bring back the money we found in our sacks last time? None of us would steal your master's silver cup."

"It's gone now," said the steward, "and it was there yesterday. One of you has stolen it!"

"If any one of us has stolen the silver cup, he shall die," they said.

"Very well," replied the steward.

The sacks were taken off the backs of the mules and opened by the steward. He began with the eldest brother. When he came to Benjamin's sack, he found the cup hidden in the corn. The brothers could not believe it. They stared in horror, and in despair they tore their clothes.

"You will have to see my master again," the steward declared.

The animals were loaded. They turned back again to the city, and arrived at Joseph's house.

Once more they bowed down before him. "What can we say? What can we do? God is punishing us for our sins. We will be your slaves."

"Only the one in whose sack my cup was found," said Joseph. "I am not going to punish you all. The rest of you may go home to your father."

Joseph wanted to know whether they would leave their brother behind in Egypt.

Then Judah went up to Joseph. "May I speak a word to you, my lord? I know that you have the power of Pharaoh himself, but do not be angry with your servant. You asked us about our father and our young brother, whom our father dearly loves. You said to us your servants, 'Bring him down.' We told you that our father would not let him come, in case anything should happen to him – he has already lost one son. We told our father we could get no more food unless we brought him, and at last we persuaded him to let the boy come.

"Our father will die if he does not return safely to him, for he is very fond of him. We cannot return without Benjamin. Besides, I promised my father that whatever happened I would keep my young brother safe and bring him back again. Therefore, please let me stay, instead of the boy! I cannot go back without him. My father would die if the son he loves so much did not come home again."

"Everyone leave the room, except these men!" Joseph commanded.

When they had all gone, he broke down and wept. The brothers were astonished. What was happening?

"I am Joseph!" he cried. They looked dismayed. They could not believe him!

"Is my father really alive and well?" he asked. They could not speak.

"Come near to me," he said, and they came near. "I am your brother Joseph whom you sold into Egypt. It was really God who sent me here to preserve life in the time of this great famine. God has made me to be Pharaoh's first minister. There are to be five more years of famine still, but we have grain stored up to save your lives. Now, go back quickly to my father and tell him what God has done! Tell him to come down here, and you bring all your families, and I will look after you. Can you not see that it is your own brother Joseph who is talking to you?"

Then he embraced his young brother Benjamin and all his brothers, and they had a long talk together.

The brothers then prepared to hurry back to tell their father that the lord of the land was none other than his son Joseph whom he had thought was dead. Joseph gave them wagons to bring all their baggage, their wives and their children to Egypt.

"See that you do not quarrel on the way!" Joseph warned.

Jacob goes to Egypt

The brothers hurried back home with Joseph's wagons.

"Joseph is alive!" they told their father, "and it is he who is the ruler of all Egypt."

Old as he was, Jacob was so glad to make the long journey to see his son Joseph in Egypt. He did not forget to thank God, and at Beersheba he stopped to worship Him.

That night, God spoke to him:

"Jacob! Jacob!"

"I am here," the old man answered.

"You may go to Egypt," God said. "I will be with you and you will be with Joseph when you die. Many children will be born to your sons in Egypt. Your family will grow and become a great nation. But, one day they will come back to this land which I have promised to give your family."

So Jacob and all his family continued to Egypt. Joseph's chariot was made ready and he went to meet his father. When they met they threw their arms around each other and Joseph wept.

Then, Joseph told the king: "My father and all his family have arrived," and he took them to see Pharaoh. Jacob blessed the king of Egypt. Then they all went to settle down in the good land of Goshen. There Joseph saw that they all had enough food to eat.

He often saw his father Jacob, who told him about God's promises to Abraham and Isaac. He also told Joseph about the times God had appeared to him. Jacob reminded his son that God had said that the family would go back one day to the land God had promised them.

Before Jacob died, he called all his twelve sons together to his bedside and talked to them about God's purposes for them. When he had finished, he blessed each of his sons, bowed his head, and died.

Joseph asked Pharaoh for permission to take his father's body back to his own land to be buried there.

So Joseph, his brothers, and many officials from Pharaoh's court all went to Canaan land to bury Jacob. Then, they returned to their families in Egypt.

Moses is born

Goshen was the part of Egypt where the family of Israel settled. More children and grandchildren were born to Jacob's sons, until there was a great number of them. The brothers grew old and died, and so did Joseph. Before he died he gave instructions that his bones should be taken back to the land of Canaan, for God had said that the people would go back there one day. It was many years before that was to happen. In the meantime, the family of Israel grew larger and larger. The children of the twelve sons became twelve tribes, and the twelve tribes became a nation. They were called the Hebrews, or the people of Israel.

Pharaoh also died, and a new king came to the throne. He did not know about Joseph, and how he had saved the people from starvation, nor how he had helped the Egyptians to become a great nation. The new king said:

"What are all these Hebrew people doing here? They are not Egyptians! There are so many of them, they might join with our enemies one day and fight against us and turn us out of our own land. Let us make them powerless. We will make them our slaves. They shall work for nothing and build great cities for us."

So that is what happened. Pharaoh put taskmasters over the people of Israel. But it made no difference. The numbers of the Israelites still grew. So Pharaoh told the taskmasters to make them work much harder! The taskmasters were cruel. They beat the slaves and gave them no rest. But still the numbers of the Israelites increased.

Pharaoh said, 'What shall we do?" So he decided to call together the midwives who helped the Hebrew women when their babies were born. He told them, "If you see it is a little boy baby, then you must kill him. But if it is a girl, she may live."

But the midwives feared God. They knew that this was a wicked thing to do, so they did not obey Pharaoh's command.

"Very well," said Pharaoh. "Here is what must be done: every single boy baby that is born to the Israelites shall be thrown into the river Nile! Only the baby girls shall be allowed to live."

That was a terrible thing to do. There was a great outcry in Israel. Can you imagine what the fathers and mothers felt when a little baby boy was born to them?

But there was one man and his wife who decided:

"We are not going to throw our beautiful little baby into the river! We will hide him." They already had a girl called Miriam, and a boy they called Aaron.

However when their new baby boy was three months old they could hide him no longer. Pharaoh's soldiers might hear him cry any day, and he would be taken to the river where he would be drowned.

The little family got together and decided what they would do. They made a basket of bulrushes and coated it with pitch, so that no water could get in. They made it comfortable for the baby, and laid him down inside. Then, his mother and big sister Miriam took the basket down to the river and placed it among the reeds where they knew that Pharaoh's daughter, the princess, came to bathe.

Miriam was left to watch what happened to her baby brother. Sure enough, the princess came along with her maids to her bathing place. She saw the basket floating on the water and sent one of her maids to fetch it. Imagine! When she opened the lid, there lay a little baby boy. He began to cry. "Oh," said the princess, "what a beautiful baby! It is one of the Hebrew children."

The princess could not bear to see such a little baby die. She took him in her arms to comfort him. She wanted to keep him for her own.

Then Miriam came up to the princess, and she asked, "Would you like me to get a Hebrew nurse to look after the baby for you?"

"Oh, yes! Go and find one!" replied Pharaoh's daughter.

Miriam went like the wind to her mother, who came and bowed before the princess, who asked her:

"Will you take this child and nurse it for me? And I will pay you wages to look after him."

How happy they were to be going home with their very own baby! They would keep him until he was old enough to go to the palace. No one would hurt him now, for he belonged to Pharaoh's daughter. She called him 'Moses' which means 'to draw out', because, she said, "I drew him out of the water."

Moses escapes to Midian

Moses the baby became Moses the boy. Then he went to the palace and was trained to be a little prince, for he was the adopted son of the princess.

Moses had the best teachers in Egypt, and he lived as an Egyptian prince. But he knew that he was really one of the Hebrew people.

As he grew older, he could not bear to see the taskmasters beating the Hebrew slaves as they toiled in the hot sun, making bricks and carrying heavy loads.

One day, when he was out he saw an Egyptian beating a Hebrew slave with his stick. The poor man was knocked down, and still the Egyptian lashed out at him. Moses' anger grew. He looked this way, and that way – there was no one about. He went up to the Egyptian and struck him such a blow that it killed him. Quickly, Moses buried his body in the sand, and returned to the palace.

Next day, Moses found out that people knew what he had done. Then Pharaoh heard, and would have killed Moses, but he escaped and fled to the land of Midian.

He was no longer a prosperous prince, but he became a shepherd and worked for a man named Jethro, looking after his sheep. Moses stayed there for many years, married one of Jethro's daughters, and a little boy was born to him whom he called Gershom.

All that time the people of Israel were still being ill-treated in Egypt. They cried to God, and God heard their cry. He had His plan and Moses was the man to carry it out. He would save God's people from slavery in Egypt, and lead them back to the land that He had promised to them.

The bush that did not burn

Moses was out in the hill country near Horeb with Jethro's sheep. He had brought them there to find pasture that was good and green. At the same time, he was on the look-out for wild animals which might come and attack any lambs that strayed away from the flock.

Moses had been away from Egypt for a good many years now. He often thought about his people back in that land. He wondered how they were. Travellers coming from Egypt would tell him that his people were still slaves there. What could he do about it? Where were God's promises to Abraham, to Isaac and to Jacob? Had God not promised that His people would go back to the land – the land of lush valleys where streams ran down from the mountains, where they would make their homes and grow their crops? Moses often thought about it, but nothing ever happened.

Suddenly, a nearby bush burst into flames. This was a strange thing to happen, but as Moses watched, there was something about that burning bush that was even more strange. Its leaves and blossoms and branches were not scorched nor shrivelled up by the heat of the flames. It was still there.

"How can that be?" Moses asked himself. He got up from the rock on which he was sitting and went to look more closely.

"Moses, Moses!" It was the voice of God that called. Moses was startled, and he said, "Here I am."

"Do not come any nearer," God said. "Take your sandals off your feet, for the ground on which you stand before this bush is holy."

Moses knew that God had something important to say to him, and he was afraid. He put his hands over his face.

"I am the God of Abraham, the God of Isaac and the God of Jacob. I have seen all the misery and distress of My people in Egypt," God said. "I have heard the cries because of their cruel taskmasters there. I am going to deliver them from the Egyptians. I am going to bring them into that good land of Canaan as I promised My people. Now, Moses, I am sending you to Pharaoh, and you are to bring My people out of the land of Egypt."

Moses was astonished, and he could not believe the words.

"Not me, Lord! Who am I, that I should go to Pharaoh? How could I possibly bring all those people, the children of Israel, out of Egypt?"

God spoke again. "I am going to be with you, Moses."

"But they will not believe me when I tell them that You sent me," Moses protested.

God said, "Pharaoh will not want to let My people go. I will have to show the Egyptians that I am God by mighty signs and wonders before they let My people go. I will give you a sign now. Throw your shepherd's staff down on the ground!"

Moses did so, and the staff became a snake which slithered along the ground and raised its head to hiss at Moses. Moses ran away from it.

"Grasp it by the tail," God commanded. Moses did so, and it became his shepherd's staff again.

Then, God told Moses all he was to do, and what he was to say.

"I can't do it," said Moses. "I'm not good at speaking. Send someone else."

Then, God began to grow angry with Moses.

"I have told you that I will be with you and will help you," He said. "I have already sent your brother Aaron to meet you and he too will help you. Get away to Egypt now and bring My people out of all their troubles. Lead them here to this mountain to worship the Lord their God."

Moses went back to Jethro. "Let me go to Egypt to see my people," he said. He did not forget to take his shepherd's staff, the staff which had become a snake. And so he made his journey to the land of Egypt.

He stayed at a lodging house one night, and there God spoke to Moses again. God repeated to him what He was going to do, and there Moses dedicated his family to the Lord God before he sent them to Jethro, his wife's father.

Moses' brother Aaron came to meet him. It had been many years since they had seen each other. They talked together for a long time about what the Lord wanted them to do.

So Moses came back to Egypt to bring his people out of the land of their slavery.

"Let My people go!"

Before going to see Pharaoh, Moses and Aaron gathered the leaders and elders of Israel together and told them that the time had come when God would deliver them from Pharaoh's taskmasters. Moses showed them how his shepherd's staff became a real snake and how it returned to his hand as his staff again. Then the people were glad. They believed that the time had come for their deliverance. They bowed their heads and worshipped God. But it was not going to be as easy as they had hoped.

Moses and Aaron went to see the mighty Pharaoh.

"We have come with a message from the Lord God of Israel," they said. "Our God wants His people to go and worship Him in the wilderness."

"Who is the Lord," demanded Pharaoh, "that I should obey him? I do not know the Lord. The people of Israel may not go!"

Moses and Aaron spoke up bravely to the king.

"The God of the Hebrews has met us and commanded us that the people shall go and worship Him. If you do not let them go, terrible things will happen."

"I have work for the people to do, and the work must be done! Go out of here and get the people back to their work!"

The Pharaoh called his taskmasters. "The Israelites are not working hard enough," he told them. "You are not to give them any more straw to make their bricks. They must find it themselves. They must still make the same number of bricks every day as they made before. If they don't, they are to be beaten!"

So the taskmasters told the people, "No more straw! Get it where you can find it!" The Israelites had to look everywhere for straw or some other material to make their bricks. "Is that all you have made today?" the taskmasters cried. "You lazy people, where are the bricks?"

"You are not giving us any straw, but you are still saying to us, 'Make the bricks.' How can we?"

Then, the brutal taskmasters lashed out at the Israelites and shouted angrily, "Get back to your work, you idle people!"

So the suffering of the poor Israelites was worse than before. The officers of the people went to see Moses and Aaron. They were angry. "It's all your fault," they told them. "We are in worse trouble now than we were before. They will kill us if we don't do the work."

Moses prayed to the Lord. "Why is all this trouble coming upon Your people? You have not delivered them out of their slavery. Why have You sent me?"

Moses and Aaron came before Pharaoh once more. "Show me a miracle – how powerful is your God?" said the king.

Aaron threw down his staff and it became a snake. Pharaoh called his magicians. "See this!" he said. "Can you do anything like that?"

The magicians went away to practise their magic. They came back. "Yes, we can," they said, and they threw down their rods which appeared as snakes. But Aaron's rod swallowed up all their rods!

"Now," said God to Moses, "it has really started. Pharaoh has hardened his heart against Me. Tomorrow, when Pharaoh goes down to the river to worship his god, you are to meet him there, and show him what I can do to his river god."

When Pharaoh came, Moses said: "The Lord God of the Hebrews has sent me to you. He says, 'Let My people go to serve Me in the wilderness.' Now, O King, you will know that He is the Lord. Look, I will strike the water of the river with my staff, and it will turn to blood."

And so it did. All the fish in the river died. The Egyptians had to dig wells to get clean water.

But Pharaoh's heart was hard – he would not listen to Moses.

A week passed by. The Lord spoke again to Moses. "Go to Pharaoh. Tell him, if you refuse to let My people go I will send swarms of frogs everywhere."

Then Aaron stretched out his hand over the land, and frogs began to come out of the Nile and from every lake and pond. They came into people's homes, climbed in their beds, and jumped into their food. They were everywhere, in houses, gardens, shops and all over Pharaoh's palace.

Pharaoh called for Moses and Aaron. "Pray to the Lord to take away the frogs, and I will let the people go."

"I shall be happy to ask God to destroy all the frogs," Moses responded. "When would you like it to happen?"

"Tomorrow," Pharaoh replied.

"Let it be as you have said," was Moses' reply. He continued, "You will know now that there is no one like the Lord our God.

Tomorrow, the frogs will die. Only in the river will they be found alive."

It happened exactly as Moses had said. The Egyptians made great, foul-smelling heaps of them.

When there were no more frogs, Pharaoh's heart was hardened. He changed his mind. He would not let the people go.

Next, the Lord sent lice which infested everybody, as well as all the animals. Everyone was itching and scratching, and trying to rid themselves of these pests. They bit the people in their beds at night, and they worried them all day. The magicians said to Pharaoh, "This is not ordinary magic. This is God's doing." But, still Pharaoh would not listen, nor let the people go.

Moses warned Pharaoh again. The next plague was of flies. In Pharaoh's palace, as well as in the homes of all the Egyptians, the rooms were thick with flies. It was horrifying. They buzzed around the people all the time. But there were no flies in the homes of the Hebrews.

Pharaoh called for Moses and Aaron once more. He promised to let the people go. Moses prayed to God. The flies departed, not one was left. But Pharaoh would not let the people go.

The Lord told Moses to go to Pharaoh and tell him:

"All your animals will die: cattle, horses, donkeys, camels, sheep. All the animals belonging to the Egyptians, but no animals of the Israelites, will die."

The very next day it happened as Moses had said.

The next plague was of boils. Everyone suffered from boils.

"Go and tell Pharaoh that there will be a tremendous hailstorm which will destroy everything," said God. It hailed everywhere, except in Goshen where the Israelites lived.

Locusts came next, and they ate up everything. Nothing green remained on the trees or plants.

Pharaoh called urgently for Moses and Aaron. "Ask the Lord to forgive my sin," he pleaded, "and I will let the people go."

Moses prayed. The locusts disappeared. Still Pharaoh would not let the people go!

Over all the land of Egypt came an awful, thick darkness. No one could see anyone else for three days. But the people of Israel had light where they lived.

Moses went to see Pharaoh for the last time. Pharaoh shouted, "Get away from me! I don't want to see you ever again."

There was one more terrible plague to come.

The Exodus

The Lord said to Moses, "I am sending one more plague upon Pharaoh. This will cause him to drive you out of the land. First, let everyone ask the Egyptians for jewels and articles of silver and of gold." The Egyptian people were glad to give the Israelites what they asked.

Then Moses called the leaders of Israel together. "On the fourteenth day of this month," he said, "at midnight, the eldest son or the eldest daughter in every Egyptian family will die, as well as all the firstborn of the animals. Now, do exactly as I tell you, and not one of you will die.

"By the tenth day of this month every home will take a lamb and will keep it until the fourteenth day of the month. Then, as it begins to grow dark, you will slay the lamb and you will put some of its blood on the sides and on the tops of the doorframes of your homes. You will roast the lamb and eat it with bitter herbs and bread made without yeast. You are to be dressed, and all ready to leave Egypt, because that night the Lord is coming. When He sees the blood of the lamb on the top and the sides of your door, He will pass over you and no one in your house will die. From now on, each year you will keep this Passover feast, to remind you that the Lord passed over you and delivered you from your slavery in Egypt."

When that night came, it happened as Moses had said it would. The firstborn, even in Pharaoh's house, was found dead. As everyone awoke, a great cry went up among the Egyptians. In every house someone had died.

Pharaoh summoned Moses and Aaron in the night. "Begone! Get all your people, and go now and serve the Lord!"

The Israelites were ready. So the great journey began. There were six hundred thousand men, besides women and children. Many other people left with them, as well as their flocks and herds. God guided them with a column of fire at night, and by day with a column of cloud. This column led them right on toward the sea which separated Egypt from the neighbouring country, and there they camped.

The king of Egypt was told. "The Israelites have gone, not one remains." Then, Pharaoh and his officers said, "Why did we let them go? We have no more slaves to do our work for us!"

"Get the chariots ready!"

Six hundred of Pharaoh's fastest chariots were assembled, together with his best horsemen. They raced after the Israelites who were by now approaching the sea. When they looked up at the end of the day they saw Pharaoh's army behind them. In front of them lay the sea. They were trapped! "We shall all die!" they cried out to Moses. "Why did you bring us out here to perish?"

"Don't be afraid!" Moses commanded them. "Stay where you are, and watch! The Lord will save you."

Moses prayed to God. "Tell the people to move on toward the sea," God instructed him. "Raise your staff over the sea. I will make a pathway for you to pass through."

At the same time the cloud which was leading them moved from the front of the line of Israelites, to the rear. It was now dark, and the cloud was so thick that the Egyptian soldiers could not find the people. On the other side of the cloud, it was all light for the Israelites.

As Moses raised his staff over the sea, a strong east wind began to blow, which drove the sea back, making a dry path for the people to cross. It blew all night long, and all that night the people marched across the sea bed until they were all safely on the other side. The water had piled up on either side of them.

As it began to grow light, the Egyptians looked and saw that their slaves had escaped across the sea. "After them!" shouted Pharaoh. The chariots drove down the path by which the Israelites had crossed over. When they reached the middle their chariot wheels became stuck in the mud.

"Quick, we must get away!" they cried. But it was too late. Moses stretched out his hand over the sea. It returned and covered all Pharaoh's men and chariots. Not one escaped; they all perished.

When the Israelites saw what God had done for them by His great power they feared the Lord, and put their trust in Moses, His servant.

Living in the wilderness

The people of Israel were now finally free from their Egyptian taskmasters. They were never to be troubled by them again. How they rejoiced that God had saved them! Moses wrote a song about God's power and how He had brought them through the sea on dry land. The people sang the song and praised God. Moses' sister, Miriam, together with all the women, danced and sang and praised the Lord.

So, the journey to the Promised Land began. They travelled with all they had brought out of Egypt – their children, their flocks, and their herds.

God had many things to teach them now. They had to learn to depend on Him all the time. Their first problem was – no water. They journeyed for three days and found no place where they could drink. At last, they did come to a place where there was water, but when they tasted it, they found it could not be drunk because it was so bitter. The people soon started to complain to Moses, who prayed to the Lord. Then God showed Moses a tree, which he cut down and cast into the water. The water became fresh and sweet, fit for all the people to drink.

Moses spoke to the people. "God will bring you to the Promised Land, but you must trust Him and do what He says. Do not be afraid. He has promised to look after us."

After that, the Lord brought them to a pleasant place where there were twelve fresh springs of water and seventy palm trees. There they camped and rested themselves.

Food was the next problem. There was not enough food in the wilderness to feed all those hundreds of thousands of people. Again, they began to complain to Moses. "We are all going to die! Why did we not stay in Egypt? We will all starve to death here in the desert."

Moses prayed again to the Lord. Then he told Aaron to gather all the people together and tell them that God had heard their grumbling. "You are complaining against the Lord your God," Aaron said. "Did not Moses tell you to trust Him? Nevertheless, God

will send you meat this evening and bread tomorrow morning."

That evening, thousands of birds called quails came flying over the camp of Israel. They landed among the tents, and the people ran and caught them and cooked them to eat.

Next morning, the people found that a kind of heavy dew had fallen all around the camp. It was like crystals of frost. "What is it?" they asked. Moses answered, "This is the bread the Lord has sent you. Gather it up. Collect it every morning. Do not keep any till the next day, as it will go bad. God will send it fresh to you every day until we reach the Promised Land."

They called the bread, 'manna'. Some kept it until the next day, when it became mouldy, as Moses had told them it would. When the sun came up it melted away, but there was more there next morning for everyone. None was to be found on the Sabbath Days. "Collect twice as much as you need the day before," Moses said, "because no manna will come on the Sabbath Day. Keep some of it – it will not go bad on the Sabbath Day."

Some people did not obey Moses. They did not collect their double portion before the Sabbath, and so they had none for the Sabbath Day.

In these ways, God showed His people that they needed to trust Him and obey Him. The children of Israel kept some of this manna in a pot, to take to the land of promise. It would always remind them of how God had fed them in the wilderness.

But the people began again to grumble. They had journeyed on and had once more come to a place where no water could be found. "Give us water, Moses," they demanded. "We are thirsty. If you don't find us any water, we will kill you!"

Again, Moses prayed. "What shall I do with this people?" he asked. "They do not believe You are with us, and will look after us."

"I will show the people that I am with you, Moses," God replied. "Call the leaders and elders of the people and go to the rock of Horeb. Take that staff with you, the one with which you struck the river Nile, and in front of all the elders, strike the rock." And this is what Moses did. He struck the rock, and out gushed water for all the people!

Moses called that place, 'Massah', which means 'contention', because the people contended with God there. He called it, 'Meribah', also, because they did not trust God, when they said, "Is the Lord with us, or not?"

So God provided for His people both food and water as they travelled on toward the Promised Land.

They camp by the mountain

Attacked by the Amalekites

While the children of Israel were still encamped at Horeb the fierce Amalekites came to attack them.

Moses called Joshua, one of the leaders, and commanded him to choose men from among the people to go out and fight off the Amalekites.

"I am going up the hill with my staff, and Aaron and Hur will go with me. I shall be holding up my hands and praying for you as you fight," said Moses.

So Moses went up the hill and Joshua and his men went out to do battle. So long as Moses held up his hands the men of Israel were driving the enemy back. But whenever Moses' arms began to ache and he let them drop down, the Amalekites began to win. So Aaron and Hur made Moses sit on a large boulder. Then, they held up his hands, one on each side. In this way, the Israelites prevailed. They held Moses' hands up until the end of the day, by which time Joshua had completely defeated the Amalekites.

Moses built an altar there to worship God Who had given them the victory.

Wise advice

As Israel was encamped by the mountain of God, visitors came to see Moses. One was Jethro, his father-in-law. He came with Moses' wife and their two sons. Jethro had heard that the people of Israel had left Egypt, and he had come to see Moses. They had a long talk together in Moses' tent, and he told Jethro all the great and mighty things which God had done, and how the Lord had looked after His people and provided food and drink for them. Jethro praised the God of heaven, and worshipped Him with Moses and Aaron and all the elders of Israel.

The next day Moses was busy from morning until night. All the people who had troubles and problems came to him. Some of them had arguments with others which they wanted Moses to sort out. So many people wanted to speak to Moses, he did not have a minute to do anything else all day long.

Jethro said to Moses, "You can't spend all your time doing this every day for all these people. You will weary yourself. It is too much for you."

Moses said, "I have to tell them what God would have them do. I have to instruct them in His way."

"Listen," said Jethro, "I know that you are God's teacher, but this is what you should do. Now, you select wise men from among the people – men who fear God, love the truth, and live good lives. Let the people bring their problems to these good men. If there is any very hard case, then let them bring the problem to you."

So that is what Moses did. Then, Jethro said goodbye to Moses, and he went back to his own home. How glad Moses was that his father-in-law had come to see him!

God speaks

The great camp of the Israelites was spread out in the plain below Mount Sinai. Moses climbed the mountain to talk with God and there the Lord God spoke to His servant Moses.

"Moses, I have important things to say to you, and I am going to talk to you on this mountain. Go down now and tell the people to wash themselves and their clothes, and tell them that they must not come up this mountain, or they will die. I am coming, and My presence will be here."

So Moses went down and called the elders together, who instructed the people. "You are God's people, He has saved you, and in three days' time He is going to tell you what He wants." The people responded, "Whatever the Lord says, we will do."

On the third day, in the morning, the people heard great claps of thunder, and there was lightning over the mountain. A trumpet sounded; so loud was the noise that it made the people tremble. There was fire and smoke on the mountain. The people were afraid. Then, the voice of God came, calling Moses to go up the mountain. Moses went up to meet with God.

The commands of God

Moses climbed up the mountain to pray to the Lord God. He stayed on Mount Sinai for a long time. There God gave him all His laws for the people to observe and obey.

There were laws about people who injure or kill other people. There were laws about servants and how they should be treated. There were laws about animals and how others' possessions should be treated. There were laws about getting married, and about people who tell lies. There were instructions about the way to treat strangers – God's people must treat them kindly. There were instructions also about keeping God's day and about special religious feast days to be kept.

Then, God promised to bless His people, to keep them and provide them with all they needed.

After that, God showed Moses how the people were to worship Him. He explained to Moses about the special tent in which they were to worship Him. God told him just how this special tent, or tabernacle, was to be made, with its beautiful curtains and poles covered in gold.

God showed Moses what was to be placed in this tent of worship. There was to be a gold box, or ark, over which cherubim of gold stretched their wings. A golden lampstand was to be made, with seven branches for seven lamps. There was to be an altar on which sacrifices were to be offered, and a table for bread which the priests were to eat. Also, there was to be an incense altar. A great bowl was to be made of brass for priests to wash themselves before entering the tabernacle. God told Moses that the tribe of Levi were to be His priests, and that Moses' brother Aaron was to be anointed as High Priest. Special garments were to be made for the priests, and Moses was given instructions on how they were to worship the Lord.

These, and many other words, God spoke to Moses while he was on the mountain. Then, He gave Moses ten great and special laws, which were written on two tablets of stone, and this is what was written on them:

I am the Lord your God. You must have no other gods but Me.
You must not worship any image or picture or statue, or anything else in heaven or earth, except Me.
You must use the name of God with reverence and respect; you will be punished if you use God's name irreverently.
Remember to keep the seventh day holy. Six days you can do all your work, but the seventh day is the day when God rested after He had made the world. Therefore, God blessed the seventh day and made it holy.
Honour your father and mother.
You must not commit murder.
You must not commit adultery.
You must not steal.
You must not tell lies about other people.
You must not long for anything which belongs to someone else.

Now, Moses had been on the mountain with God for many days. Had he forgotten the people? They came to Aaron and said, "We can't wait all this time for Moses to come back from the mountain. We need some kind of god."

They brought all their wives' golden earrings to Aaron and he had them melted down and made into a golden calf. Next day, the people held a feast and began singing and dancing before their new god.

Up on the mountain, God spoke to Moses, "Your people whom you brought out of Egypt have turned away from Me and have made themselves an idol." God was very angry. "I will destroy this people," He said.

Moses prayed to the Lord. "You can't do this. What will the Egyptians say? They will say, 'You brought them out in the wilderness only to kill them!' Besides, Lord, remember Your promises to Abraham, Isaac and Jacob."

Moses hurried down the mountain to see what was happening. When he saw what the people were doing, he threw the stone tablets down, and they broke in pieces. He then took the golden calf which they had made, and ground it to powder. He confronted his brother Aaron: "Whatever made you let the people do this?" he demanded. "God will punish us for this." That very day, three thousand men of the Israelites died. Then Moses said, "I will go up the mountain again to beseech the Lord God, to see if He will forgive you."

"If You will not forgive them, then blot me out of Your book," he prayed.

God's answer was to promise Moses that He *would* forgive the people, and that He would take them on to the land He had promised to them.

The last days of Moses

Moses spent a long time with the Lord God on the mountain. While Moses was there, the Lord also gave him many rules and laws for the good of the people, as well as instructions about the way they were to worship. God said to him, "Cut two more tablets of stone, and I will write My words again on these tablets.

"I am going to send my Angel before you and I will drive out all your enemies, and I will give you a good land in which to live. But I will not go with you, for you are such a disobedient people."

When the people heard that, they were dismayed because the Lord would not go with them.

Moses pleaded with God. "If Your Presence will not go with us, do not send us on from here. You must go with us."

The Lord answered, "You have found grace in My sight and I know you. I will do as you have asked. I will go with you."

"Please show me Your glory," prayed Moses. "I want to know that You are really with us." Then Moses saw the glory of the Lord as He passed by.

Now, when Moses came down from Mount Sinai with the two new tablets on which God's law was written, his face shone with the glory of God. The people were afraid to come near to him. He then told them all that God had said.

The people gave to Moses the precious things they had brought out of Egypt. From the gold and the silver and the precious stones they began to make the ark, the holy table and the candle holder, all of gold. They made all the curtains for the tent of worship and for the courtyard around the tent. From the silver they made the posts and pegs. They made the great bronze washing bowl, and the altar of sacrifice; also, the beautiful garment for Aaron the High Priest, with its breastplate of sparkling jewels.

When all was ready, and everything was put in its place, the cloud of God's glory rested above the tent, and filled it. The cloud of the Lord was always above it by day, and fire glowed over it by night wherever the people of Israel went.

Moses taught the people God's way and prayed for them. They chose leaders from their tribes and began to move on toward Canaan. Their journey took them through the mountains of the Amorites and then across the great wilderness plains until they came to Kadesh-Barnea on the borders of the promised land they were to enter.

Moses sent one man from each of the twelve tribes into the land to find out what it was like.

After forty days they came back with a great bunch of grapes and other fruit. The men said, "It is a good land the Lord is giving us, but there are giants there and the cities are strongly fortified. We cannot hope to defeat them."

Then Joshua and Caleb said, "With God's help we are able to overcome them. Come on, let's go at once in the name of the Lord God."

But the people were afraid and turned away. Aaron and Moses were greatly distressed and fell down on their faces and prayed to the Lord. The people had come to the land, but would not go in. So they wandered about in the wilderness.

Meanwhile, God had to teach them many things. The Moabites came to attack them. Snakes bit them when they grumbled, and God punished them when they rebelled against His prophet Moses.

So, after many years, the Israelites arrived back again at the border of the land which God had promised to them. Moses knew that he did not have long to live, and he knew that he would never go into the Promised Land now. He spoke his last words to the people. He told them that God had given them the land and that they were to enjoy it. He warned them that if they disobeyed God they would be punished. Enemies would come and take them away captive. Moses also told them that a greater prophet than he would come to them one day. He then blessed all the people and appointed Joshua to lead the people into the land God had promised them.

After these words, Moses left them, climbed Mount Nebo to look out over the land to which God had brought his people, and there he died. For thirty days Israel mourned for Moses. There had never been a man like him before. Moses had brought the people out from slavery, had spoken all God's words to them, and brought them to the Promised Land.

Crossing the river

Before Moses died he had appointed Joshua to lead the people into the Promised Land. Moses had gathered the people together and had called Joshua out in front of them all. "You are the chosen one to take these people into the land God has promised to His people. The Lord your God will go before you, He will lead you and the land shall be yours. Be strong! Be courageous! Do not be afraid. God will be with you, He will not leave you."

Then Moses had given the book of the law of God which he had written to the priests to look after. "This must be read to all the people so that they and their children will learn to love and fear the Lord their God in the land."

But now Moses, that great leader of God's people, was dead. Joshua was worried. But how good it was to know that God was going to be with him as He had been with Moses! So Joshua summoned the leaders of the tribes of Israel.

"Get ready to cross the river," he said. "The Lord is with us," they responded. "We will obey you, as we obeyed Moses."

Joshua sent spies across the river to find out about the city of Jericho. They found the city fortified and prepared for any attack which might be made. They were seen, but a woman named Rahab, who believed that the Lord God was with the people of Israel, hid them. The spies promised that her house would be saved and everyone in it. After dark she let them down the outside of the city wall by a rope, and they escaped back to report to Joshua. The men of Israel would know her house by the scarlet rope hanging from her window on the city wall.

The spies told Joshua, "The Lord is certainly going to give us all the land; the people are worried. They are all afraid of us!"

The next morning, the camp moved on toward the river Jordan. The river was flooding over its banks. How were they to get across, with all the children and their baggage, as well as their flocks and herds?

Joshua instructed the people. "When you see the ark of God

carried by the priests, follow it. Camp here tonight, but tomorrow be ready, and see what the Lord your God will do, and you will know that He is with you."

Joshua spoke to the priests. "Take up the ark of God and cross over the Jordan river. Everyone will walk over on dry land."

The priests marched right up to the river. Then, as soon as their feet touched the water, it stopped flowing. There was no more water coming from up river, and that which had been flowing ran away downstream. The priests moved out into the centre of the river bed and stayed there with the ark until every single person had crossed over. Before the priests came out of the river Joshua called twelve men. "Bring twelve boulders out of the river, and make them into a pile. When your children ask, 'What are they there for?' tell them, 'This is to remind us how God brought us across the river into the Promised Land.'"

So this was done, and as soon as the priests came up out of the river bed with the ark of God, the waters flooded back and overflowed the river bank as before.

God had shown the people that He was with Joshua as He had been with Moses.

Now, when the people of the land heard that all Israel had crossed over the Jordan river they were even more afraid. They shut the gates of their cities and prepared themselves to face the people of Israel.

In the distance stood the fortified city of Jericho. This was the first place they must overcome. Joshua wondered how his army could ever get inside those stout walls. He went for a walk toward the city, in order to think about it. He looked up, and there standing before him was a man. The man had drawn his sword.

"Are you for us, or for our enemies?" brave Joshua demanded.

"I am come," was the answer, "as Commander of the Army of the Lord." Joshua realized that it was the voice of God. He fell down on the ground, and worshipped Him.

"What does my Lord want to say to His servant?" enquired Joshua.

"Take your sandals off your feet, for where you are standing is holy," came the answer. Joshua did as he was commanded.

Then God showed Joshua what he had to do to capture Jericho.

Jericho falls

The men of Jericho looked out toward the camp of Israel. They were not sure what was going to happen. Their city was surrounded by a great wall. It was very thick. It was strong, it was high. However could those people from the wilderness knock it down? The gates of the city were stout, and they were closed fast. No one could get in. Their fighting men stood at the top of the walls ready to ward off anyone who tried to climb into the city. The guards were on watch night and day. It was true that there were a great many people in the camp of the Israelites, but they did not look as fierce as the armies of the other nations. Besides, they had all their wives and children with them.

Yet the men of Jericho did not feel easy. They had heard what the God of Israel had done. Had not all these people been Pharaoh's slaves in Egypt? Had not their God opened up the sea for them to escape, and had not Pharaoh and all his soldiers and horsemen been drowned when they tried to follow? Had not Israel defeated the Amalekites also? Moreover, their God had supplied them with food and water in the wilderness, and led them by a cloud in the daytime, and a warm glowing fire by night. The inhabitants of Jericho could see that very cloud above the Israelites' tent of worship.

What would the God of the Israelites do now? Somehow, they had all managed to cross over the Jordan river in full flood.

The men of Jericho were worried. Fear was in their hearts as they watched the camp of Israel. Were they safe in their strong city?

Now, the Lord God had told Joshua what to do. "The city is yours," God had said. "The king and all his mighty men will be defeated. This is what you will do.

"The priests will take the ark to the city and march around it once. Seven priests will take rams' horns with them. These are your trumpets to blow with a loud sound. Behind them, more priests will carry the ark of God. You will all march right round the city once. Then, you will come back to camp. That is all you will do. The next day, you will do the very same thing."

The men of Jericho saw Israel coming. They prepared to defend their city. They saw the priests and the ark. They heard the piercing sound of the rams' horn trumpets. They watched Joshua leading his men around the city, and they saw them return to their camp. What did it mean?

The next day, the same thing happened. The priests came, the ark was carried on their shoulders around the city wall; the trumpets blew, and they went back again. This happened in the same way each day, for six days. Every day the Israelites brought the ark. Every day the seven priests blew the seven trumpets.

On the seventh day it was different. The men of Israel marched around the city once, but they did not go back. They marched around it a second time. There were men all around the city, each one with his sword or spear.

Round they marched a third time. Seven times they tramped around the city. Joshua had told his men to say nothing until he gave the command. As they came around for the seventh time, Joshua cried, "SHOUT! for the Lord has given you the city!"

Immediately, a great shout went up from all the men of Israel. The earth trembled beneath them, the walls of the city began to crack and crumble with the shaking. Then they fell down flat! All was confusion. Every man of Israel could now go straight into the city.

Now, God had said that it was such a wicked city that everyone and everything had to be destroyed, and so this is what the men of Israel did. Everything in the city was destroyed. Only Rahab and her family were spared, as the spies had promised. The Israelites saw the scarlet rope outside her house, and all her family were saved and came to live with the people of Israel.

It was the first great victory in the land. Later on, songs were sung about the great victories of Israel. Here is part of Psalm 47:

'O clap your hands, all you peoples!
Shout to God with the voice of triumph!
For the Lord Most High is awesome;
He is a great King over all the earth.
He will subdue the peoples under us,
And nations under our feet ...
God has gone up with a shout,
The Lord with the sound of a trumpet.
Sing praises to God, sing praises!
Sing praises to our King, sing praises!
For God is the King of all the earth.'

What happened at Ai and Gibeon

The defeat of Jericho was a great victory for Israel. The city was burned with fire. Joshua ordered that nothing was to be taken from it by the people, except things of silver or gold, bronze or iron. These were to be used for the house of God.

But one man did disobey Joshua. His name was Achan. The Lord God was angry that any of His people should be disobedient.

The next city to be taken was not far away. It was called Ai, and Joshua sent some men to see what kind of a city it was. When the men came back, they said, "It is only a small city, you need not send everyone up there, we can take that city easily." So Joshua sent only a small army there to fight against the men of Ai. But the men of Ai came out to fight the men of Israel, and the Israelites were beaten. Thirty-six men were killed, and the rest turned and ran for their lives.

When Joshua heard what had happened, he tore his clothes and fell down before the ark of God and prayed: "O Lord God, what has happened? All the people of the land think we are weak; they will now attack us. Are You not with Your people? Why has this happened? We shall all be killed."

The Lord said to Joshua, "Stand up! There is someone sinful in the camp. Someone has taken spoil from Jericho city for themselves, which I said they should not do. This is why you have lost the battle of Ai. I will not be with you until that one is punished."

Joshua addressed the people. "Tomorrow," he said, "you will all appear before me in your tribes and in your families."

Early next morning all the twelve tribes were assembled before Joshua. After looking at them all, he picked out the tribe of Judah. "The guilty one is someone in this tribe," said Joshua. Looking at the people, he pointed at one family and said, "It is someone in this family." All the family stood before Joshua, and from it the man Achan was taken. "What have you done?" demanded Joshua. Then the man confessed.

"When I was in Jericho I saw a lovely Babylonian garment, some

silver, and a wedge of gold. I coveted them and I took them and hid them in the earth under my tent."

Joshua sent men to Achan's tent and there they found the loot, which was brought before Joshua and laid out before all Israel. "Why have you troubled us?" asked Joshua. And they stoned Achan and all his family, and all their possessions were burned.

Then the Lord told Joshua how he was to take the city of Ai, so the men of Israel went a second time to Ai.

The men of Ai did not know that Joshua had sent most of his men to hide in the country behind the city. As some of Joshua's men approached the front of Ai, the men of the city came out as before, to chase the Israelites away. When they had left the city, the men in hiding came into Ai from behind and set fire to it. Looking back, the men of Ai were aghast to see their city burning. They were then surrounded by the Israelites who won a great victory.

After this victory, Joshua built an altar on Mount Ebal and the children of Israel worshipped the Lord their God there. Then all the words and commands that God had given to Moses were read out to all the people.

When the kings of the tribes in the land heard that the people of Israel had taken Jericho and the city of Ai they began to be afraid. Five kings gathered their armies and advanced on Gibeon, for Joshua had made peace with the men of Gibeon. The Gibeonites sent a messenger to Joshua asking him to come and help them.

Joshua's mighty men marched through the night and came upon their enemies suddenly. They attacked them, and before long the armies of those five kings began to run away. Then Joshua commanded his men, "Do not let them get away, chase after them, and catch them, before it gets dark."

The battle was not over when Joshua cried, "Sun, stand still!" and God caused the sun to stop in its course until Israel had defeated her enemies. There had never been such a day before, when God, to help His people, stopped the sun from going down. So the men of Israel won the day and returned to their camp to rest.

One by one, Joshua conquered the tribes occupying Canaan. It took the people of Israel many years to win the land which God had given to them. At length, Joshua divided up the country among the twelve tribes of Israel. So the people spread out and settled in the land which God had promised to Abraham, Isaac and Jacob long ago.

The Judges

In his lifetime, Joshua had defeated thirty-one kings in the land of Canaan; he was now an old man. He called all the elders of Israel together to Shechem. He said to them: "The Lord your God has given you this land. You now have rest from all your enemies round about. You have all been allotted places in the country, where you are to live. Now you must keep all God's laws which He gave to Moses. If you disobey Him, the Lord will no longer keep your enemies out of the land He has given you."

Joshua reminded the people of all the good things God had done for them and all the good gifts He had given them. "If you forsake Him and serve other gods, trouble will come upon you," he said. They replied, "The Lord our God we will serve, and His voice we will obey."

Then the people went to their homes and their fields, and soon afterward Joshua, the servant of the Lord, died at the good old age of one hundred and ten years.

The years went by. When the young people had grown up, they forgot all that the Lord God had done for them, and they began to worship the gods of the people who lived in the lands round about them. Raiding parties began to loot their villages and farms, and took the people away captive, as the Lord had said. Then the people of Israel began to cry to the Lord to deliver them. So God appointed some leaders, called judges, to deliver His people Israel from their enemies. But the years went by, and again they forgot about their God.

Once more, their enemies descended upon them, stole their produce, ill-treated them, and made God's people work for them. In their distress, the people of Israel cried out again to God. Then God chose other judges who saved the people and brought them back to the ways of the Lord. There were Othniel, Ehud, Shamgar and Deborah. All these judges were raised up by God to deliver His people from their enemies.

The people obeyed God and served and worshipped Him, but after a time they forgot the Lord again, and did evil in His sight.

Gideon

The people of Israel were in trouble again. They had sinned against their God Who had saved them from Egypt and given them the good land of Canaan. Because of this, God allowed the Midianites to attack them. The people of Israel sowed their wheat, but as soon as it was cut the Midianites would swoop down and take it all away. So the Israelites had no wheat to make their bread.

There was a young Israelite named Gideon, whose father was a farmer. One day, he said to his son, "We have our wheat harvested and have put it where the grape vines grow, to hide it from the Midianites. Go and thresh it so that we can have flour to make bread. But keep watch for the Midianites!"

Gideon was threshing the wheat in the vineyard when suddenly the Angel of the Lord appeared and spoke to him. "The Lord is with you, you mighty warrior! Go in all your strength and save Israel from their enemies!"

Well, Gideon was not feeling much like a warrior. What could this mean? He answered the angel, "If the Lord is with us, why has all this happened to us? The Lord used to be with us, but not now. He has left us." The Lord replied, "I will be with you, and you will defeat the Midianites."

"But, Lord, however can I save Israel? My tribe is the weakest of all the tribes of Israel, and I am the youngest in my family. Prove to me that it is really the Lord Who is commanding me," Gideon said. He added, "I will bring an offering to You." And so he did. He placed his offering of meat and bread on a rock. The angel touched it with his staff, and fire came and burned it up, then the angel departed. By this sign, Gideon knew that it was God indeed who was speaking to him, and he worshipped the Lord his God there in the vineyard.

The first thing he had to do in order to show that he was God's man, was to destroy the idol which stood outside his father's house. That night, the idol was pulled down, and then Gideon built an altar to the Lord.

Now Gideon was ready to fight the Lord's battles. Soon the Midianites and the Amalekites crossed the river Jordan and prepared to attack Israel. Then the Spirit of the Lord came upon Gideon. He blew a trumpet and sent messengers to gather the men of Israel to battle.

As the army of Israel approached, the Lord said to Gideon, "There are too many men here. The people will say, 'It was because the army was so strong that they won the battle.' I want to show everyone that you won because the Lord is with you. Now, announce to the men, 'Anyone who is afraid, may go home again.' "

Twenty-two thousand people went back home again. This left only ten thousand men. "There are still too many," God said. "Bring them down to the brook to drink. Those who take up a handful of water, put aside. All the rest who get down on their hands and knees for a long drink – send them away." By this test God was able to choose those who were anxious to go into battle without delay. Now there were only three hundred men left to fight against the Midianites. Could they defeat that great army with only three hundred men?

This is what they did. That night, Gideon gave each man a trumpet and an earthenware pitcher. He gave them each a lighted torch which they put in the pitcher to hide its light. Then, Gideon's men spread out all around the hills surrounding the army of the Midianites as they camped in the Valley of Jezreel. Gideon said, "When I begin to blow the trumpet, you all blow your trumpets. Then, when I shout, you shout. When I break my pitcher, you break yours."

And this is what they did. Gideon blew the trumpet, and all the trumpets sounded out. Then, he shouted, "The sword of the Lord, and of Gideon!" And all his men shouted, "The sword of the Lord, and of Gideon!" They broke their pitchers. Three hundred burning torches appeared all around the camp. This frightened the Midianites. They thought that their enemies were upon them. They seized their swords and in the darkness and confusion began to fight one another. Finally, they left their camp, and ran. The army of Israel pursued them all next day and chased them out of their land. Once more, God had saved His people from their enemies.

Samson

Yet once more the people of Israel forgot all about their God, and how good He had been to them. They began again to worship the gods of the heathen people around them. As a result, God allowed their enemies to oppress them. The Philistines became their masters, and that lasted for forty long years. This time, it was Samson who was God's man to deliver the Israelites from their enemy.

It always made the women of Israel sad when they had no children. For many years, Manoah's wife had no baby. Every day she prayed to God and asked Him to give her a baby boy. At last, God heard her prayer. The Angel of the Lord appeared to her and announced, "You are going to have a son. He is to take the vow of a Nazarite. He is never to have wine, nor take strong drink, and he must not eat food that is unclean. Neither must his hair be cut. God will use him to begin to deliver the people of Israel from their enemy, the Philistines."

Manoah's wife told her husband about the angel, and what he had said. Manoah prayed to the Lord, "Please let the man come and see us again; we want to know how we should bring up this child that shall be born." The angel did appear again. Then, Manoah's wife ran to fetch her husband, and the angel talked with them both. Manoah and his wife brought an offering of grain and a young goat, and they worshipped God. As they did so, the angel ascended in the flame of the altar. Manoah and his wife never forgot that day. They knew that it was the Lord Who had spoken to them. In due course, the baby was born, and they called him Samson.

Samson grew to be a fine young man, sturdy and very strong. He liked playing jokes, but he had a bad temper. Samson annoyed everyone. He liked beautiful women, and this made more trouble. Nevertheless, God used Samson to deal with the enemies of Israel.

One day, he said to his parents, "I have seen the girl I want to marry." His parents were not at all pleased, because she was a Philistine girl who belonged to Israel's enemies. "Could you not find a young woman from among God's own people?" they asked him.

But Samson was determined to marry only her.

As he was going to Timnath to see his bride he came to some vineyards. A young lion appeared and roared at Samson. He had no weapon in his hand, but the Spirit of the Lord came upon him in a mighty way. He killed the lion and tore it apart with his bare hands, and left it there. Some time later, he saw that a swarm of bees had made a nest inside the lion's carcass. He took some of the honey home with him, but Samson told no one about the lion.

At his wedding Samson had thirty young Philistine men as companions. He asked them a riddle. "If you can give me the answer I will give you thirty sets of clothes," he said. "Good," they answered, "tell us the riddle." It was about the lion and the honey:

"Out of the eater, came something to eat,
Out of the strong, something sweet."

For three days the young men tried to think what it meant. On the fourth day they went to Samson's wife. "We cannot think what it means," they said to her. "We are all going to look foolish. You are his wife, he will tell you everything – ask him what it means."

So she kept asking Samson to tell her the answer. "You are keeping secrets from me," she said, and she began to cry.

Samson said, "I have not told anyone that, not even my father and mother." The wedding feast lasted a week, and his wife kept worrying Samson to tell her. Finally on the last day, he did tell her, and she then went to tell the young men. So, right at the end of the wedding festivities, they came and said to Samson, "What is sweeter than honey? And what is stronger than a lion?"

Samson was angry. He knew that his wife must have told them the answer, so he went out and killed thirty Philistines, and gave their clothes to the young men who had found out his riddle. Then, he left without his wife.

Later, when he came back for her, her father said, "Now you cannot have her. I have given her to someone else." This made Samson even more angry with the Philistines. He went out and burned all their corn which was drying in the fields, as well as their vineyards, and their olive groves.

"Who did this?" they asked. When they discovered it was Samson who had destroyed their crops, they killed his wife and her father. "Now I will have revenge!" Samson raged, and in fury went to slaughter more Philistines.

So the Philistines gathered their army and marched against Israel.

"Give us Samson, or we will destroy you," they demanded.

Then the people went to Samson: "You are the cause of our

trouble!" they said. "We are going to take you to the Philistines; we have come to take you."

"I will not resist," said Samson, "but do not kill me yourselves." So they promised.

They bound him up with new ropes and took him to the army camp. When the Philistines saw Samson, they began shouting at him. Then, the Spirit of the Lord came upon Samson; he saw on the ground the jawbone of a donkey. He broke the ropes binding him as if they had been bits of burnt straw, took hold of the donkey's jawbone, and laid into the Philistines singlehanded. He killed a thousand men with that weapon.

So by himself, Samson defeated the Philistine army. He became the judge of Israel for twenty years.

One day, Samson went to the city of Gaza and stayed the night there. He was not afraid of the men of Gaza, but they said, "We have caught him in the city now. At daybreak we will kill him."

During the night, Samson tried to leave the city. But the great gates of the city were locked and barred, he could not get out. That was no problem for Samson. He took hold of those gates, wrenched them out with their posts, put them on his shoulders, carried them up to the top of a hill, and left them there.

Samson loved a woman called Delilah, and he went often to see her. Now the Philistines knew about this, and they went to see Delilah. "Can you find out why it is that Samson is so strong?" they asked. "If you can get him to tell you his secret, we will give you eleven hundred pieces of silver." This was a lot of money.

So Delilah agreed to help them. The next time she saw Samson, she whispered to him, 'Tell me what makes you so strong?"

Samson said to her, "If they bound me with seven new bow-strings, I should become weak like other men."

Delilah told the Philistines, and they brought her seven new bow-strings. She managed to tie up Samson with them.

'The Philistines are here!" she shouted.

But Samson broke the new bow-strings as if they were pieces of straw.

"You lied to me," Delilah protested, "Come – tell me why are you so strong?"

"Bind me with new ropes," said Samson. "I would then be like other men." While he was asleep, Delilah tied him up with new ropes.

Then she cried, "The Philistines are here!" Samson broke those ropes off his arms, as if they had been as thin as thread.

But Delilah would not give up. "Why don't you tell me?" she cried. "You say you love me."

So Samson told her that if his hair was tied to a post he would be weak like other men.

When he was asleep, she tried this, but this time he pulled the post out, and was ready to fight any Philistine who might appear.

"How can you pretend to love me," Delilah chided, "when you keep secrets from me? Why don't you tell me what makes you so strong?"

Then at last he told her the truth. "I made a vow to God never to cut my hair. If I am shaven, I shall be like any other man."

This time, she saw that he had really told her the truth. She sent for the Philistines. "Bring the money," she said.

When Samson was in a deep sleep with his head on her lap, she called a man in to cut off his long hair. Then, she screamed: "The Philistines are here!" Samson jumped up and shook himself, as he had done before. But he did not realize that the Lord had left him.

The Philistines, who were waiting outside, rushed in, overpowered him, and took him away. They took out his eyes and put him in prison, chained him up with great chains of brass, and made him grind corn for them.

In prison, Samson's hair began to grow again.

The day came when the Philistines held their feast to the god Dagon. All their nobles gathered in the great temple to celebrate the capture of Samson. They praised their god Dagon, and cheered and worshipped him. Then, they said, "Bring Samson, and let us have some fun with him! He is blind now, and cannot see what he is doing."

There were about three thousand people in the galleries, and they all laughed and jeered at Samson as he was led in.

Then Samson called to the Lord, "Give me strength again just this once, O God!" He asked the lad who was leading him, "Let me lean on the central pillars of the temple. I need to rest." He was led to the two centre pillars and stood between them.

Then, Samson put out his hands, braced himself against them, and prayed, "Lord, let me die defeating the Philistines!" After that, he pushed with all his might.

The people did not realize what was happening until it was too late. They cried out as the pillars moved. Masonry and great stones began to fall, the roof and the walls caved in with a tremendous crash, and the temple of Dagon was no more. Samson had killed more Philistines at his death than he had done in all his life.

Ruth and Naomi

It was during the days when the judges ruled in Israel. There was a famine as God said that there would be, if His people disobeyed Him. No rains came. No wheat grew. The people were hungry.

Elimelech and his wife Naomi talked about it. "Our two boys are not getting enough to eat. They will not grow healthy and strong. They will be weak and undernourished, and they may even die. What shall we do?" they cried.

"I hear that things are better in the land of Moab," said Elimelech. "Let's go there."

"And leave our people and our relations, and all the friends we know?" enquired his wife. "Besides, they worship other gods there."

"Do you want our boys to be ill and die?" Elimelech questioned. "We will come back when the famine is over."

So Elimelech sold his house and land, packed up his belongings, left Bethlehem where he and his family lived, and made his home in the land of Moab.

After several years, Naomi's husband died, and she was very sad. But her two boys were with her. They grew up, and married two Moabite girls – one called Ruth, the other, Orpah. Then, first one and then the other of Naomi's sons died. Poor Naomi! She was grief-stricken. There was now no one to look after her, and she was in a foreign land. Naomi did not know what to do. She spoke to Ruth and Orpah.

"You both find new husbands," she said, "and I will go back to Israel, where I have relations and where I can worship the God of Israel."

Both Ruth and Orpah loved Naomi, the mother of the young men they had married. "We will come with you," they said.

"No, no," replied Naomi, "stay where you are among your own people – it will be hard for you to live in another country."

Orpah and Ruth were very sad – they cried and kissed their mother-in-law. Then, Orpah said, "Yes, I suppose it is better to stay with my own people," and that is what she did.

But Ruth said to Naomi, "No, I will come with you. I want your God to be my God. I want to worship the Lord with your people. Do let me come with you!"

So Naomi and Ruth left Moab and travelled on until they came to Bethlehem. When they arrived, Naomi's old friends said, "Is this Naomi? What has happened to you?"

Naomi said, "My dear husband and my two fine sons are dead. But Ruth has come back with me."

Now, it was the beginning of the barley harvest. As the reapers cut the stalks, some fell off and were left behind at the edge of the field. The poor people were allowed to collect these grains after the reapers had stacked the sheaves. So Ruth said, "Let me go and get some of the grain for ourselves."

The field in which she gleaned the corn belonged to a rich farmer named Boaz. When he came to the field he greeted the harvesters – "The Lord be with you!" They called back to him, "The Lord bless you!" He was a good man, and he noticed this new girl in his field. He asked his foreman who she was, and he said, "That is Ruth who has been so kind to Naomi, and left her own country to look after her."

So Boaz spoke to Ruth. "I have heard how good you have been to Naomi since your husband died. Help yourself to all the corn the reapers leave, and when you are thirsty you can drink out of my water jars. May the Lord, the God of Israel, reward you as you have come to trust Him."

At meal time, Boaz called Ruth. "Come and share some of my food," he said, and she took some home to her mother-in-law, as well.

Naomi was excited when Ruth came back with so much grain. She was even more pleased when she heard that Ruth had gleaned in the fields of Boaz. "He even told his servants to drop some stalks especially for me to pick up," Ruth told her mother-in-law.

"The Lord bless him," cried Naomi. "How good God is to us! This man is a close relative of ours. He may be able to help us."

So Ruth went back to glean corn in Boaz' field every day.

When Naomi had left Bethlehem her husband had sold his land. The Jewish law said that a person could always buy his land back again. But Naomi had no money.

At the end of the harvest, Boaz had a feast in the evening for all his workers, and Ruth was there too. After the feast, Boaz lay down to go to sleep. In the night Ruth woke him, and because he was a near relation of Naomi's she asked him to redeem (or buy back)

Elimelech's property for them. Boaz said, "I will see what can be done in the morning."

Ruth went home and told her mother-in-law what had been said, and so they waited to see what would happen.

Boaz went to see some men in the city to make arrangements. They reminded him that if he wanted to buy Elimelech's property for the family, he had to marry Ruth, too – and that is just what he did!

How happy everyone was! And when, later, a baby was born to Boaz and Ruth, they rejoiced. This baby grew up and became a father, and then a grandfather. One of his grandsons was David, who became the great king of Israel. But that is another story.

The story of Hannah

"Why are you crying?" Elkanah asked his wife Hannah.

Now, Elkanah had two wives. His other wife, Peninnah, was unkind to Hannah and made her life a misery. Also, poor Hannah had no children but Peninnah had many children, both boys and girls. Elkanah loved Hannah, but still she was unhappy and longed every day for God to give her a son.

Each year the family went to worship the Lord before the ark of God in Shiloh. Elkanah provided a feast for the family, but Hannah did not want anything to eat. She went to the tent of worship to pray, and to ask God again if He would not give her a son. Eli, the High Priest, was sitting at the door. He saw Hannah kneeling down and looking upwards. Her lips were moving but no words came. Tears ran down her face. She prayed for a long time. Eli thought that she was acting strangely and that she had been drinking too much wine. He rebuked Hannah and told her to go away and not to get drunk.

"I have not drunk wine nor any strong drink," she said. "I am a very unhappy woman. I am crying to God. I have no son."

Then Eli understood that she was grieved in her heart. He blessed her and prayed for her. "God has heard your prayer," he said. "Go in peace," and Hannah went away, sure that God would answer her prayer.

The next day was the last day of their visit. The family rose early, worshipped before the ark of God, and made their way back to their home in Ramah.

Not long after that, Hannah was so happy – she knew that her baby was coming. At last, a boy was born.

"I will call him Samuel, because it means 'God heard'. When he is old enough I will give him back to the Lord, to serve in His house. I will dedicate him to the service of God."

Now, Elkanah continued to go every year to worship the Lord at Shiloh. When the boy Samuel was able to make the trip, Hannah went again with her husband. They took an offering of thankfulness to the Lord, and they saw Eli.

"I am the woman who prayed for a son," she told him. "This is the boy for whom I prayed. I am now giving him to you for the Lord's service," and in her happiness she praised the Lord and prayed to Him.

Eli's sons were evil men. God was angry with them. But Samuel grew into a fine lad, who loved God and obeyed His laws. Every year his parents went to worship before God at Shiloh, and every year Hannah took a new coat for her son Samuel.

Eli was growing old and Samuel was always helping him in the service of the Lord. One night, when the lad had finished all his work, and before the lamp of God in the tent of worship went out, he lay down to go to sleep. All was quiet, then he heard a voice calling his name: "Samuel". Samuel got up and ran to Eli to see what he wanted.

"I did not call you, my boy, go and lie down again."

Then the Lord called him again: "Samuel". He ran to Eli's bed. Eli said, "I did not call you. Go and lie down again."

A third time, he heard his name called: "Samuel". A third time he ran to Eli. Then it was that Eli realized it was the Lord Who was calling Samuel. He said, "When you hear your name called the next time, say, 'Speak, Lord, for Your servant hears.'"

And that is what Samuel did. "Samuel, Samuel," came the voice once more. Trembling, Samuel said, "Speak, Lord, for Your servant hears."

So God spoke to Samuel, and told him what He was going to do.

Then everyone in Israel knew that Samuel had been chosen by God to be His prophet, for God spoke often to Samuel after that, and Samuel became the judge of Israel.

God punished Eli's wicked sons. They died in battle, and when the news came to old Eli that his sons had died, and that the ark of God had been captured by Israel's enemies, the Philistines, Eli was so shocked, he fell off his seat. His neck was broken, and he died.

The people of Israel had been defeated, and the ark of God was taken because they had failed to worship and to live as the Lord their God had directed them.

Samuel told the people this and he instructed them in the ways of the Lord. So they put away their other gods and asked Samuel to pray for them. Then, they began to defeat the Philistines once more.

A king for Israel

Samuel lived at Ramah, and he judged the Israelites for many years, during which time God blessed them and kept them safe from their enemies. Samuel travelled around the towns and cities, visited the people and taught them God's ways.

One day the elders of Israel came to Samuel. "You are getting old now, Samuel, and there is no one else like you to look after the people. We want a king, just like all the other nations."

"We are different in Israel," Samuel answered them. "Our king is the Lord. He has always looked after us when we obeyed Him. Do you not want the Lord God to be your king now? If you have a king he will be like the kings of other nations. He will want to keep a trained army, and your sons will have to serve as soldiers. A king will want lots of servants and horses and chariots. He will require you to give him the produce of your farms, and you will have to pay him heavy taxes."

They took no notice of Samuel's words. "We want a king," they repeated. Samuel prayed to the Lord, and then he agreed to find them a king.

There was in the land a rich and powerful farmer whose name was Kish. He had a son who was very tall, handsome and strong. His name was Saul. One day, Kish sent his son out to find some of his donkeys which had wandered away over the hills. But Saul and the servant who was with him could not find the donkeys anywhere over the mountains. Then at last they met a man who said to them, "Yes, I know where your donkeys are. They have been found. You may be looking for donkeys – but the people of Israel are looking for you! You are to be their king!"

That man was Samuel. God had told him the day before that the next day He would send to Samuel the person who was to be king. Samuel would meet him and would know just who it was to be.

You can imagine Saul's astonishment. He was even more surprised when Samuel took him into a great dining hall where there were about thirty other guests waiting for him. He was given the place of

honour at the table, and the best cut of meat to eat.

He stayed with Samuel that night. Next morning, Samuel poured some oil on Saul's head to show tht he was the one anointed to be king of Israel. The Lord God filled Saul with His Spirit, and he returned to his home, having found the donkeys.

After this, Samuel called all the people together. He reminded them of how God Himself had saved them and delivered them from all their enemies. He reminded them that they had now asked for a king like the other nations, and that God was not pleased because they did not trust Him to look after them. "Nevertheless," Samuel said, "I have found you the king you are to have." Saul was called out from among all the people and presented to them. All could see him because he stood taller than anyone else in Israel. So Saul was proclaimed the king of Israel.

When the Ammonites came to make the people of Jabesh Gilead their slaves, Saul called men from all Israel to drive them out, and a great victory was won. There were many more skirmishes with Israel's enemies during Saul's reign.

But the Lord God was not pleased with Saul. Because he did not always obey the Lord, he was not a happy man. He became irritable and miserable, especially when Samuel told him that God had now rejected him as Israel's king, and that another person would be chosen in his place.

One day when Saul was feeling particularly unhappy his servants said to him, "If some sweet music were played to you, it would make you feel better. Let us find a skilful player of the harp, and when you feel unhappy he can play for you, and you will be cheered up."

"Yes," said Saul, "find me someone who can play well, and bring him to me."

A servant said, "I have seen one of the sons of Jesse, and he plays the harp beautifully. His name is David, the shepherd boy."

So they brought young David to Saul, and from that time he used to play on his harp for the king whenever Saul was depressed.

David and Goliath

David loved to sing and play his harp. He also wrote a great many songs. We call them psalms. Christians still read and sing them in church today. They show us how much David loved and trusted God.

When David was not playing his harp at Saul's palace, he worked as a shepherd boy on his father's farm. He was a fine looking lad, could run fast, and he was very strong and brave.

One day, a bear came and took one of the little lambs out of his father's flock of sheep. David ran after the bear, fought with him, and killed him. Another time, a lion stole one of the lambs. Brave David caught him by his hair, killed the lion and saved the little lamb.

The day came when David met giant Goliath. The Israelite army had gone to fight the Philistines. David's three eldest brothers went to the battle. The Philistines were always making trouble for Israel at that time. They raided their farms, burned their grain, and took away their cattle and possessions, killing and injuring the people.

One day, David's father, Jesse, called David. "I want you to go with the servant and take these ten cheeses and this corn meal to the captain for his fighting men, and see how your brothers are."

David rose early next morning and leaving someone else to look after the sheep, he set off to the battlefield. He found the armies facing each other in the valley of Elah, shouting their battle cries. Leaving the servant with his bags, he ran to find his brothers. As he was talking with them he heard a great voice coming from the enemy ranks. A huge man clad in a brass helmet and with his body and legs covered with armour, was standing in front of the army. With a large sword at his side, a long spear in his hand, and a shining shield in front of him, he looked a terrifying sight. His name was Goliath of Gath. His voice boomed out, and everyone listened.

"Which one of you will dare to come and fight against me? I defy the armies of Israel!" he cried. "Why are you all standing there? Just send me a man and we will fight together. If he is able to fight with me, and kill me, then we will be your servants, but if I kill him you shall all be our servants and serve us."

Now, all the men of Israel were afraid of Goliath. Not one would dare go out to meet him.

David looked around at Saul's army.

"Is no one going to fight this Philistine?" he asked. "Is there no one who trusts God to help him defeat this man?"

David's brothers were not very pleased with him for asking such questions. His eldest brother Eliah was very angry.

"What did you come here for?" he demanded. "Who is looking after our sheep? You only came to see the battle. Why don't you go home again!"

But David continued to ask, "What are we going to do about that man who is speaking against us and our God?"

The king had promised the man who would fight with Goliath that he would let him marry his daughter, and he would give him riches and honour, as well. Saul heard about David, and sent for him.

"If no one else will fight this man, I will go!" said David.

The king looked at David.

"A young fellow like you cannot fight a man who all his life has been trained, like this terrible man, to battle and to war!"

Then David told Saul about the bear and the lion, and how God had saved him out of their claws.

Then Saul said, "You cannot go like that. You had better take my armour." So David tried on Saul's helmet of brass, his coat of mail, and Saul's own sword.

Said David, "I am not used to wearing all this heavy armour. I cannot fight this way," and he took it all off again. Taking his staff in his hand, he made his way out in front of all Saul's fighting men and came down to the brook which ran between the two armies. There he chose five smooth stones which he put into his shepherd's bag, and advanced toward giant Goliath.

Looking down on the young fellow, Goliath scowled as they came steadily nearer to each other.

Goliath stopped. "Do you suppose that I am some kind of a dog," he roared, "that you come to me with that stick?" – and he cursed David by his gods.

Then David spoke up.

"You come to me with your sword, and with your spear, and with your shield; but I come to you in the Name of the Lord God of Israel, Whom you have defied. Today you will be delivered into my hands, you will be struck down, and I will cut off your head. Everyone will know that there is a God in Israel. He will give you into our hands!"

These were bold words. David did not stop to talk with Goliath any more, but straightaway ran toward him. Taking a stone from his bag he put it in his sling and with a mighty swing he let fly at the giant. His aim was true. The stone hit Goliath on his forehead with such force that immediately he fell flat on his face onto the ground.

Then David ran forward, stood on top of the Philistine, drew Goliath's own sword, and cut off his head, as he had said he would.

The watching Israelites were amazed, and shouted with a great shout. The Philistines, seeing their champion was dead, turned and ran away, with the men of Israel in pursuit. It was a great day of victory for Israel.

King Saul made David the shepherd boy captain over his men of war.

All the people loved David and that day Saul's son, Jonathan, became David's great friend.

Saul is jealous

The enemies of Israel seemed always to be attacking them while Saul was their king. He sent David out as his commander to fight the tribes who came up to war with Israel. Everyone loved David, but Saul was becoming jealous of the young man. He was angry when the women met David coming back from the battle. They would sing and dance and play their tambourines. As they danced, this is what they sang:

'Saul has slain his thousands,
David has slain his ten thousands!'

Saul said, "They are singing and saying that David has done better than I – they will be wanting him, rather than me, to be their king soon!"

Next day, Saul had one of his bad moods, so David played to him on the harp. But Saul was feeling so hateful in his heart that the music did not do him any good, and his jealousy of David was very great. His spear lay by him; suddenly, he snatched it and threw it at David. But David moved too quickly for him, and darted out of his way. After that, Saul was afraid because he saw that the Lord was with David.

"I know what I will do," he said to himself. He told his servants to let David know that the king was pleased with him. "Tell him," said Saul, "that if he can kill one hundred Philistines he may marry my daughter, Michal."

Now Saul thought that David himself would be killed before ever he could kill as many as a hundred Philistines. But David went out and killed two hundred Philistines, and came back alive and well. So he was married to Michal who loved him very much.

Saul was even more afraid of David now. Surely the Lord was with David, and helping him – and everyone loved David.

Saul spoke to his servants and to Jonathan, his son, and told them that he wanted David to be killed. Saul hated David, and he could not bear that everyone should like him. Jonathan, who was David's good friend, came to him and said, "My father wants you to be killed. Be on your guard!"

One day when Saul was feeling angry again about David who had just won another battle with the Philistines, he could tolerate David's presence no longer. David was playing music before Saul when the king suddenly took another lunge at David with his spear. The spear stuck in the wall, and David escaped to his house and his wife. "You had better get away," she told him. "My father surely means to kill you." That very night Saul sent his men to take David, but he had gone.

He went to Samuel at Ramah, and told him all about Saul. As soon as Saul heard that David was there he came after him again, but David had fled from there also. He then met his friend Jonathan who promised to help him. So David and Jonathan vowed to be friends and to help each other, whatever difficulties might come.

When Saul heard that Jonathan was a good and true friend to David he was very angry and hurled his spear at his own son to kill him. But again, he missed.

Jonathan then held a secret meeting with David. He told David that his father was more angry than ever. David had to keep away. They were both sad to have to separate. Tears were in their eyes as they prayed to the Lord God, and promised to be true to each other.

So David left his friend and escaped to hide in the hills and valleys of Israel. He came to a cave called the Cave of Adullam, and there many came to join him. Soon, he had four hundred men with him, and they protected the farmers' property whenever the Philistine raiding parties came to plunder and destroy the crops.

But David could not stay in one place because Saul's men were looking for him. One day, Saul was out with three thousand of his warriors. Saul came to a deep cave and took off his cloak and rested. Now David and some of his men were hiding further back inside the cave. David's men whispered to him, "This is your chance to kill Saul – let's go and do it now."

"No," cautioned David. "It is the Lord God who has anointed him king. I cannot kill the one God has anointed."

Then David crept quietly up to where Saul had put his cloak and cut a piece from one corner.

Later Saul picked up his cloak, and went off with his bodyguard to join the rest of the army.

David came out to the entrance of the cave and called to Saul. He bowed down to the king. "My lord, do not believe those who tell you that I want you dead," he cried. "You can see that I do not mean any harm to you. My men urged me to kill you. Look at your cloak, you will see there is a piece cut off the corner. I have it here."

Saul realized that David had spared his life. He wept and thanked David, then he returned to his home.

One day, news came to David that Saul and Jonathan had both been killed in a battle against the Philistines. David was heartbroken. He wrote a song of sadness in memory of his dear friend Jonathan.

He and his men then marched to Hebron where they were reunited with their wives and families. There the people anointed David king of Israel, in place of Saul.

King David becomes great and sins

When David became king he had many problems. He wanted all the people to work together so that the nation might be secure under God. The Philistines were defeated, and God blessed David and made the kingdom of Israel great. His throne was moved from Hebron to Jerusalem, which came to be called the City of David. The ark of God was brought back and the people rejoiced. They had a great feast, and David worshipped the Lord.

Then David said to Nathan the prophet, "I am living in a fine house, but we do not have a proper temple for God in which we may worship Him." God answered David by his prophet. "I have not needed a great temple all these years, but one shall be built. You shall not build My temple, David, because you are a man of war. Your son, who will be a man of peace, shall build My temple after you have died. Your family and your kingdom will be blessed in the days to come." On hearing these words the king worshipped the Lord, and thanked Him for His kindness to him and his family.

David and his mighty men fought and won more victories. So his kingdom grew and prospered.

It was then that David decided not to go out with his men. He stayed in the comfort of his home in Jerusalem. Perhaps he was getting a little lazy. While his men were away fighting he went up to the flat roof of his house one evening and saw a very beautiful woman washing herself. He thought to himself, "I would like her to be mine."

God's law says that we must not want other people's wives or husbands for ourselves. David did wrong, and disobeyed God's law. The woman's name was Bathsheba and her husband, Uriah, was away fighting David's battles. David sent his servant to ask her to come and see him. Then he loved her, and sent her back to her house.

A little while later, Bathsheba found that she was going to have a baby. She sent her servant to tell David, "Bathsheba is going to have a baby – and you are its father, because she went to bed with you when her husband was away fighting the Lord's battles."

So David decided, "I will send for Uriah so that he may sleep with his wife, then it will appear that the baby is his, and no one will know that I took his wife whilst he was away."

But Uriah said, "No, I will not sleep with my wife while my fellow soldiers are out there fighting the Lord's battles." So David had to think again.

So he thought of another idea. He would write a letter to Joab, his commander-in-chief in the army. In the letter he wrote: "Put Uriah in a dangerous place when you attack, so that he gets killed." And so it was done.

This was a very wicked idea for David to have, and a very wicked thing for him to do. By this means, he had Uriah killed, and he was able to take Bathsheba to be his wife.

God was angry with David, as we shall see in the next story.

Nathan talks to David

Joab received David's letter. In it David instructed his commander to besiege the city he was attacking, and to put Uriah in the hottest and fiercest part of the battle. Then he was to withdraw from the battle, and leave him there. So Joab sent Uriah and his men where the enemy was strongest. They came out of the city and fought against Uriah. Others shot arrows from the city wall. They killed some of the men of Israel, and brave Uriah.

Joab sent a report back to David. The messenger was to tell the king that some men had died, and that Uriah had also died. David did not ask, "Why did you go so near the city wall with only a few men?" No. Instead, he said. "Tell Joab not to worry too much. We must expect some men to be killed. Tell him that he will overthrow the city when he attacks it next time."

Now David could have the wife of Uriah as his wife, which was the reason that he had wanted Uriah to be killed in battle. God was not pleased with what David had done.

When Bathsheba heard that her husband had been killed she mourned for him. Afterwards, David took her into his house and she became his wife, and the baby was born to him and Bathsheba.

Nathan the prophet came to see David one day. He said, "I want to tell you about two men, David. One was rich; he had a large farm, and plenty of everything. The other was poor, all he had was one little lamb. He loved this little lamb, it came into his house, he fed it from his own table, it played with his children, and he would nurse it on his lap.

"One day, a visitor called on the rich man who had lots of sheep and lambs of his own. Instead of taking one of his own lambs to make a dinner for his friend he took the poor man's lamb and left him with nothing."

When David heard this he was angry. He said to Nathan, "As the Lord lives, the man who has done this deserves to die. Besides that, he shall give that man four times as much as he took because he had no pity." David was so cross, he went red in the face.

"David" – and Nathan looked him straight in the eye as he spoke, "You are that man! The Lord God of Israel says to you, 'I have made you king over my people Israel. I have saved you out of many dangers. I have given you victories over your enemies, and I have made you rich and prosperous. You have a good family and faithful servants. Have I not given you enough? Why have you disobeyed My commandment by arranging for Uriah to be killed in battle, and taking his wife to be your wife? You will be punished, and everyone will know. Because you have taken Uriah's wife to be your wife there will be trouble in your family because you despised Me. You did it secretly, but all will see what will happen to you and your family.'"

Then David knelt down before Nathan the prophet. "I have sinned against the Lord," he said.

"God will spare your life and He will forgive you," Nathan promised. "You shall not die, but your baby who is born to you will certainly die. The enemies of God are laughing because of what you have done. It has brought terrible disgrace on the Lord God and His people."

Nathan left David and went to his own house.

The little baby born to Bathsheba did become ill. David was very sad, and he prayed and prayed to God to make him better. He ate no food and lay all night on the ground. The baby did not get better. David's servants tried to comfort him and persuade him to eat.

After seven days the baby died. The servants were afraid to tell the king that his baby had died. They thought it would make him feel even worse than he already felt. They said, "When the baby was alive we could not comfort him at all, what will happen when we tell him that the baby has died? He may do himself some harm if we tell him."

When David saw his servants whispering together he knew that his child had died. Then he asked them, "Is he dead?" They answered, "Yes, he is dead."

Then David got up from the ground, washed himself, changed his clothes and worshipped the Lord. He returned to his house and had a meal.

David's servants said to him, "Your baby has died; you wept and cried when it lived, but now it has died you are no longer sad."

David said, "When he was still alive, who could tell whether the Lord would be gracious to me and make the child well? But now he has died, he cannot be brought back again. One day I shall go to him, but he will not come back to me."

So David comforted his wife Bathsheba after their baby had died. Then God gave them another son. They named him Solomon.

The Lord God sent David's friend, the prophet Nathan, to him with the message that the Lord loved Solomon, and would bless him. So his other name was Jedidiah, which means, 'loved of the Lord'. Solomon was to become the most wonderful king that Israel ever had.

Absalom tries to be king

Absalom was David's favourite son. He loved Absalom. Absalom was a very attractive young fellow – handsome, with lovely long hair. When it was cut once a year it weighed about five pounds.

Nathan the prophet had told David that there would be trouble in his family, and there was. Amnon was a half-brother to Absalom. One day, Amnon ill-treated Absalom's sister, Tamar, and made her very unhappy. Absalom would not forgive his half-brother Amnon, and when the opportunity came, he killed him. His father, the king, and all the family were very sad and wept bitterly.

Absalom ran away. According to the law, he should have been punished, and in fact, he should have died for what he did, but his father did not want him to die. After three years, the king agreed that he could come back to Jerusalem, but David would not see him, although Absalom wanted his father's forgiveness. After another two years, he did ask Absalom to come and see him. Absalom bowed down before his father, and the king kissed his son.

Everybody liked Absalom. He was really good looking and had great charm. Absalom thought that he was now a person of importance in the kingdom. He provided himself with a fine chariot and horses, and had fifty men to run in front of him. He wanted to be king of Israel.

He used to get up early in the morning and stand by the road leading to the city. People came from all over Israel and he talked to them. "If I can help you," he said, "let me know." So he made friends with many people from different parts of the country. They thought he was a nice, kind man.

When he thought that he had gained many friends who would be on his side, he invited two hundred of them to a feast in Hebron. During the feast his close friend made a proclamation: "Absalom is king!" The trumpets sounded, and Absalom sent messengers throughout the land, saying: "Absalom is king!"

The people were then quite convinced that this was true. Absalom's servants and friends took their swords to fight anyone who did not want to accept Absalom as their king.

King David's faithful servants told him what was happening, and said to him, "We must get out quickly, before they come to kill us!" So King David, and all the men who were faithful to him, made their escape from Jerusalem. All the people who loved David wept when they saw him being forced to leave the city. A man named Ziba gave him and his men donkeys, carrying bread and raisins, figs and wine.

As soon as David's men had left the city, Absalom and his followers entered Jerusalem and shouted, "Long live the king!"

Then, Absalom's chief adviser encouraged him to chase after his father and to kill him, but Hushai, another counsellor, who was really on David's side, said, "No." Hushai then sent David a message secretly to let him know what was happening. So David was able to get right away. Other friends provided him and his men with flour, vegetables and cheese, and they were able to rest from their journey.

Soon, many more men came to join King David. Plans were made to defeat the rebellion and bring the proper king back to his throne in Jerusalem. They prepared for battle. David gave special instructions to Joab his commander: "Be gentle with the young man Absalom, for my sake." All the troops heard David's instructions that his son Absalom was not to be killed.

The time came for battle. Both sides met in a valley by the forest of Ephraim and there was a great conflict between the men of Absalom and the men of David. The battle spread out and into the forest. As Absalom was on his horse galloping through the forest, a low branch caught his head and his long hair. He was swept off his horse which ran on without him.

Some of David's men saw him hanging there and they told Joab. "Why did you not kill him?" cried Joab.

"You heard what the king said," replied one of the men. But Joab did not listen. He ran with his armour bearers, and they killed Absalom where he was, hanging from the tree.

Joab sounded the trumpet to announce that the rebellion was over.

A messenger came to tell the king that the battle was won. "Good news!" he said. "God has defeated those who rebelled against you."

David wanted to know, "Is the young man Absalom safe?" The messenger replied, "May all those who rebel against you be like that young man!"

David realized that the son he loved was dead. He bowed his head in grief and went to his room and wept. "O my son, Absalom! My son, my son Absalom," he cried, "if only I could have died instead of you. O Absalom, my son, my son!"

Now Joab and his men and all the people who loved David were glad that the victory had been won for their king. They were glad also that David and his family and all his followers were saved. But when they heard that their king was grieving, they were sad, too.

Joab went to see David. "If you do not come and speak to the people who have helped you and fought for you," he said, "they will not want to follow you."

David's heart was so heavy and he was very sad, but he roused himself and went out to see his faithful people.

Solomon becomes king

King David's faithful friends welcomed him back to Jerusalem and the people realized that he was the true king for Israel. The kingdom settled down in peace as the last of their enemies were driven away in the years that followed. David the king grew old. Solomon was the son who was born to David's wife Bathsheba, and it was he who was to be the next king, by the Lord's choice.

But another son of David, called Adonijah, Absalom's brother, said to himself, "My father is old now. The country needs a new king. I will be king." He prepared chariots and horsemen for himself. He also asked his father's general, named Joab, and Abiathar the priest to help him. Then, he held a great feast for all his friends and proclaimed himself king.

David's faithful friends and Solomon's mother went to King David and said, "Did you not say that your son Solomon was to be king after you?"

"Yes," replied David, "it is to be Solomon. Put him on my horse; blow the horn, let all the people know. Sit him on my throne, and proclaim: 'Long live King Solomon!' "

The people were glad to know that Solomon was to be king and they rejoiced with great joy, and danced and played their flutes.

When Adonijah heard the noise, he said, "Is that for me?"

"No," they said, "King David has made Solomon king and he sits on the throne."

Adonijah and his friends were now afraid of what the new king would do to them. They ran away.

Not long after that, King David, who knew he would soon die, called his son Solomon, and gave him his final words: "Walk in God's ways and obey His words."

Then David's life came to an end. For forty years he had been a good king in Israel, and had brought peace to God's people.

Now Solomon loved the Lord, and the Lord blessed him. One night he had a dream. In his dream the Lord God appeared to him. "What shall I give you? Ask whatever you like."

Solomon did not ask to become rich or powerful. He did not ask to defeat his enemies, or any of those things. He said, "You have been very kind to me, and to my father David. Now I am not very old, and You have asked me to look after all these people. I need wisdom and understanding if I am going to be a good king and Your servant."

God was very pleased with Solomon and He said, "As you have not asked to be rich and powerful, I am going to give you what you asked for. But, I will give you riches and honour as well. There will never be anyone so wise and understanding as you will be!"

Next day, Solomon went to worship before the ark of God, to thank Him for His kindness.

Soon everyone began to see just how wise and understanding Solomon was. His kingdom prospered. He traded with other lands and made friends with other nations. Instead of fighting, they helped one another. Kings and men from other countries learned about Solomon and came to hear his wisdom.

"Now," said Solomon "is the time to build the temple of the Lord in Jerusalem." He sent word to Hiram, his friend, who was king of Tyre, and asked him to send hundreds of cedar and cypress logs. Great stones were cut and conveyed from the quarries and many men were engaged for many months to build the great temple. Everything was overlaid with pure gold, all the rooms and the stairs, as well as the holy places. The altar and all the carved decorations, as well as the huge cherubim, or angels, were carved in wood and covered with gold. Also, palm trees and flowers were made. Even the floor was of gold. It took seven years to finish the work. A great bronze bath, or bowl, rested on the backs of twelve carved oxen, and there were ten other baths in which there was water for washing. Solomon made a golden altar as well as the seven-branched lampstand for the temple.

When it was finished all the people were called to come to the temple, and Solomon prayed a great prayer of thanks to God. He prayed for the people also, that they would not depart from the way of the Lord, and he prayed for the people who would come from other lands to see the temple, and worship the God of Heaven.

Not long after that, someone did come to see Solomon and the temple. It was the Queen of Sheba. She arrived with all her servants and talked with Solomon. He explained to her how the true God should be worshipped. She saw his palace and all his servants, and heard his wisdom. She said, "It was a true report I heard about you in my country, but they did not tell one half. It has taken my breath away! Happy are your people," she said, "the Lord God has been good to you and has given His people a good king."

Solomon wrote a lovely song about how much God loves His people. He also wrote down many of his wise sayings. They are called Proverbs. Here is one of them: "Trust in the Lord with all your heart, and lean not on your own understanding."

Elijah and the wicked king

Solomon was a good king during the first part of his reign, but when he became rich and wealthy he did not entirely obey the Lord. He married foreign wives and began to worship their gods. The Lord was angry with Solomon, and said to him, "I will take the kingdom of Israel from your family and leave your son to be king over one tribe only. Another king will rule over the rest of Israel."

When Solomon died his son, Rehoboam, reigned over Judah, and one of Solomon's mighty men became king of Israel. Other kings followed, and some of them were evil. In time, Ahab became king of Israel. His wife Jezebel was even more wicked than he was. The people forgot their God and they began to worship the heathen god, Baal.

Nevertheless, God loved His people and raised up prophets to speak His words to them, to bring them back to Himself again. The prophets told the people that if they did not turn back and worship the one and only true God, trouble would come upon them – and so it did.

One day, the prophet Elijah appeared before King Ahab. His message was short and sharp:

"As the Lord lives, before Whom I stand, there will be no dew or rain until I say."

The Lord said to Elijah, "Go and hide by the brook Cherith, it will give you drink. Every day, the ravens will come and bring you food." Elijah obeyed the word of God, and God sent the ravens. Every morning and every evening they brought fresh bread and meat for Elijah to eat.

Because there was no rain, the brook dried up. God said to Elijah, "Go to Zarephath. There a woman, who is a widow, will look after you."

As Elijah came to the city he saw a woman collecting sticks. "Please bring me some water and a little bread," he asked her.

"As the Lord your God lives," the lady replied, "I have only a handful of flour left. I was just collecting these sticks to light my fire and bake a little loaf of bread for myself and my son. It will be our last meal before we die."

"Do not be afraid. Do as I say, and you will find that your flour will not be used up, nor your oil run dry, until the Lord sends rain again."

So the lady and her boy did not die, and Elijah stayed with them many days, until it happened that the lad became ill. His mother was distraught to see him so unwell. As she held him in her arms, his breathing stopped.

"What have I done that my son should die?" she cried.

"Give me your son," Elijah said. He carried him up to his room, laid him on the bed, and earnestly prayed to God: "Why has this happened? Will You be gracious and give this child's life back to him?"

Elijah stretched himself out on the child three times. The boy moved, came alive, and was revived. Elijah took him downstairs to his mother. How happy she was as she took him in her arms again! "Now I know that you are a man of God!" she exclaimed.

It had not rained for three and a half years. Water was scarce and crops did not grow. Ahab the king had sent his servant Obadiah out to find a place where his horses could get some water to drink. Elijah went to meet him, and said, "Tell King Ahab that I am coming to see him."

When Elijah met the king he said, "You have been worshipping Baal. Your wife Jezebel has been helping the false prophets of Baal, and she has been killing the prophets of the Lord God.

"Gather all Baal's prophets on top of Mount Carmel, and we will see who is the true and real God."

Four hundred and fifty prophets of Baal came. Elijah said, "Here are two bulls for sacrifice. One for you, and one for me. Here we will build two altars and sacrifice the bulls on them. We will put no fire under them. The God Who answers by fire and burns up the sacrifice without our putting any fire under it, He is the true God!"

The prophets agreed.

"There are many of you – so have your chance first," Elijah said.

So they prepared their sacrifice. Then they called on their god Baal to burn up the sacrifice. "O Baal, hear us!" they all prayed. Nothing happened. They kept calling out to their god; they leapt on the altar. Elijah waited.

"Shout louder!" he mocked, "perhaps he is busy, or has gone away. Or maybe he is asleep. Shout louder!"

In the afternoon the prophets began cutting themselves with knives

until their blood gushed out – but it made no difference. Their god paid no attention.

It was the time of the evening sacrifice. Then Elijah said, "Now everyone come near!"

He took twelve stones, one for each of the twelve tribes of Israel, and built up the altar. He laid the sacrifice on the altar, he put the wood under it. He dug a trench all around. Then he said, "Pour water on the sacrifice and the wood."

They did so.

"Do it again."

Three times they did it, and water ran into the trench and filled it.

The people watched quietly. Elijah prayed: "Hear me, O Lord, that the people may know that You are the Lord. Turn their hearts back to You again."

Then the fire fell on the sacrifice. The wood, the stones, and the water in the trench all disappeared in the fire.

The people fell down and worshipped God. "He is the Lord!" they cried.

"Seize the prophets of Baal!" Elijah ordered. They were all executed.

Then the people saw a small cloud. Soon the sky was black with clouds; the wind blew, and it began to rain. It rained and rained. The people had returned to their God, they were once more able to grow their crops, and provide food and drink for man and beast.

But King Ahab and his wife Jezebel remained as bad as ever. One day the king saw a vineyard belonging to a man named Naboth, and he wanted it. So Jezebel arranged to have Naboth put to death. Then Ahab took possession of the vineyard.

God sent Elijah the prophet to Ahab. "You, your wife and your sons will die violent deaths," he declared – and they did.

None of Israel's leaders had done as much evil as Ahab and Jezebel.

Elisha follows Elijah

Elisha was ploughing his field one day when the prophet Elijah came to find him. Elijah took off his cloak and threw it over the shoulders of Elisha, and walked on.

In this way, Elijah was telling Elisha that he was to follow him and become the next prophet of God to Israel.

Elisha ran after Elijah and said, "Let me tell my family and say 'goodbye' to them, and I will come and be with you." Elisha made a feast for his people from the oxen who had pulled his plough, and then he left to serve Elijah. For several years he learned the ways of God from the prophet.

The day came when Elijah was to be taken up to Heaven by a whirlwind. He set out on his last journey. Elijah said to Elisha, "Stay here, I am going to Bethel."

"I am coming with you," Elisha said. When they arrived there the student prophets (groups of men who followed their ways) said to Elisha, "Do you know that the Lord is going to take your master away today?"

"Yes, I know," he said.

Elijah said to Elisha, "Stay here, the Lord is sending me to Jericho."

Elisha refused to leave him. "I am coming with you," he replied. At Jericho the student prophets there said to Elisha, "Do you know that the Lord is going to take your master away today?"

"Yes, I do know," he said.

Elijah said to Elisha, "Stay here, the Lord is sending me to Jordan."

Again, "I am coming with you," Elisha answered. So they went together. Fifty student prophets followed them.

When Elijah came to the river Jordan, he took off his cloak, rolled it up, and struck the water with it. A pathway appeared, and the two prophets walked across on dry ground.

The two men talked together. "What shall I do for you before I am taken away?" asked Elijah.

"Please give me a double portion of your spirit," responded Elisha.

"If you see me go, you shall have what you have asked for," Elijah replied.

Elijah was giving his young friend his final words when the parting came. Elisha saw the whirlwind and the chariots coming for Elijah. "My father, my father!" he cried. "The chariots of fire and the horses!" – and Elijah was gone.

Elisha picked up Elijah's cloak which had fallen from him, and went back to the Jordan river. "Where is the Lord God of Elijah?" he called, and struck the river. It divided, as before, and he walked over. Elisha now knew that the Lord was with him, as He had been with his master Elijah.

The student prophets met Elisha. "Where is Elijah?" they asked. They went to look for him, but could not find him anywhere. Then they knew that Elisha was now the prophet of God to His people.

God now worked various miracles through Elisha as the Lord had done through Elijah, so the people knew that he was God's prophet.

One day the wife of one of the student prophets came to Elisha. "My husband, who reverenced the Lord, has died," she said. "My husband owed a man some money, and now he wants it back. I do not know what to do for I have no money. Now the man says that he is going to take my two boys as slaves."

"How much food have you in your house?" Elisha enquired.

"Your servant has nothing in the house, except for a jar of oil," she replied.

"Then," said Elisha, "Go and borrow from your friends as many empty jars, jugs and bowls as you can. Take all they have. Then take your sons indoors with you, and begin to pour out the oil from your jar into all the jars, jugs and bowls you have collected."

The woman did as he said, and began to pour the oil out into one jug and then another until she had filled them all to the brim. "Bring me another jar," she said.

The boys replied, "There are no more jars."

Then the oil stopped flowing.

The woman went to Elisha and told him what she had done and what had happened. Her house was full of pots of oil.

"Right," Elisha said, "Go and sell the oil and you will have enough to pay your debt."

Naaman

Now Naaman was the commander of the army of the king of Syria. He was a great man and had won many victories for his king. Once his raiding party had brought back some captives from Israel. Among them was a little slave girl, and she became servant to Naaman's wife. Naaman was a good commander and a brave man, but he had one thing wrong with him. He suffered from a terrible skin disease which gradually rots skin and bones.

The little girl said to her mistress, "If only my master Naaman could be with the prophet Elisha, who lives in Samaria where I come from – he would heal my master of his leprosy."

Naaman's wife told her husband what the little girl had said. "Tell me about this man," Naaman said, and she told him all about Elisha.

Next, Naaman told the king of Syria, who said, "I will write a letter for you to the king of Israel. Take money and presents also."

So Naaman made the journey and arrived at the king's palace. The king of Israel did not understand how he could possibly have Naaman cured. He thought the king of Syria was trying to quarrel with him.

When Elisha heard about Naaman, he said, "Send him to me." So Naaman's horses and chariots, with all his servants, stopped outside Elisha's door. Elisha's servant answered the door and came back to Naaman with a message.

"Go and wash in the river Jordan seven times and you will be completely healed."

Naaman did not like that. In fact, he was very angry. He expected the prophet to hold a great ceremony with all the priests and say special prayers and wave his hand over the diseased parts of his body.

"Why should I not wash in the rivers in my country? Are they not much better than the waters of Israel?" So he went off in a rage.

Then his servants spoke to him. "Sir," they said, "if the prophet had told you to do something great, you would have been glad to do it, wouldn't you? But because he did not make a great fuss over you, you don't want to do what he says."

So Naaman decided that if he wished to be made better he should do as the prophet said. He went to the Jordan river and dipped in its waters seven times. When he came up the seventh time his skin was as smooth as a child's. He was overjoyed. He went back to the man of God to thank him. He told the prophet that from now on he would worship the Lord only.

Naaman offered Elisha the gifts he had brought with him. "No," said Elisha. "I do not want any presents. Go in peace." So Naaman bid him goodbye, and left for his home.

Amos, the shepherd preacher

After Elijah and Elisha, the Lord God sent other prophets to His people to warn them that they would be invaded by their enemies and carried away captive to other lands if their wicked ways continued.

Amos was not one of the sons of the prophets. He was a shepherd and looked after sheep in the hills near Bethlehem. But God called Amos to speak His Word to the people. Many of them had become wealthy and were living in luxury, but others were very poor. Those who were rich were unkind and cruel to the poor. They stole their corn. There was bad language and violence, and people killed one another. Some were taking other people's husbands and wives. Besides all this, they were worshipping Baal, and they followed the wicked ways of the other nations. God sent Amos and his friend the prophet Hosea to tell the people that unless they changed their ways their country would be invaded. Their grand buildings would be destroyed, their soldiers would be defeated, their fortresses would fall, and their cities would be burned. Disaster would descend upon them; the enemy would take all their fine clothes and break up their lovely homes and lead them away with hooks in their lips to become slaves in a foreign land.

Amos preached to all the nations around Palestine, but especially to the northern kingdom of Israel, and its capital city of Samaria, with its beautiful palaces. He told them the day would come when they would no longer be lazily listening to their music on couches and feasting themselves every day with the best meat and wine.

The prophet Amos prayed for the people of Israel twice, and God heard his prayer and did not bring destruction upon them at that time. But the people continued in their ungodly ways. Amos boldly continued to preach to them. They did not like it, and said to him, "Get out! And go back to Judah where you came from – do your prophesying there."

"I will do that," replied Amos, "and your land will fall into the hands of the enemy. You will die of hunger and thirst, some of you will be killed by the sword, and the rest will be taken to die in another country."

The people of Israel did not listen to God's prophet. It hurt Amos to see the wickedness of the people; he was so sad because they did not listen to his warnings.

He had one final word to say. It was a word of promise. He told them that God would one day, in years to come, bring some of them back again. Their land would be fruitful once more, and they would come back and worship the Lord in the land He had given them.

Isaiah and the army of Syria

God did just as the prophet Amos said He would do. The armies of the Assyrians came, destroyed the kingdom of Israel, and led away captive the people who survived. This left Judah, with its capital Jerusalem. The Assyrian empire had grown stronger. At any time Judah and Jerusalem might be attacked.

Isaiah was God's prophet at that time. He had many things to say. He told the people about their sins, not only his own nation but also the nations around them. Isaiah warned them what was going to happen to them, and all he said came true. Also, he told the people about the One who was to come, the Messiah. He was to be born in an unusual way, He would be called Immanuel, which means 'God with us,' and He would be a servant of God and would suffer for His people's sins. At the same time, He would be great, and His kingdom would extend over the whole world. How did Isaiah know all this?

He was in the temple of God one day, when he had a vision of the Lord God. Isaiah realized that God Himself had something to say to him. He felt very sinful in God's presence. "Your sin is taken away," the voice said. Then Isaiah heard the Lord speaking. "Go and tell the people My words. It is I who send you." So Isaiah did as the Lord told him.

Some years later, the king of Assyria did come and attack the land of Judah and took its inhabitants away, but Isaiah said that the enemy would not come into the city of Jerusalem. God promised to protect Jerusalem at that time.

Hezekiah was king. He was a good king and loved God, and he listened to His prophet Isaiah. One day a messenger brought news that the great Assyrian army was on the move. They were marching toward Jerusalem, and sure enough they came, one hundred and eighty-five thousand men. They camped outside Jerusalem.

The commander of the army had a message for the king of Jerusalem, so Hezekiah's messengers went out to meet the commander.

"Tell Hezekiah that Sennacherib the great king of Assyria says, 'How do you think you can stop me from destroying your city and taking all its gold away? Have I not conquered every other city and taken it? Have not my gods helped me? Do you think your God is going to prevent me from defeating your city? Look at this great army here, all ready to fight. Let us make peace. If you will be our servants and come to our rich country, all will be well.'"

Hezekiah's messengers pretended not to understand. So the commander shouted to the people looking over the wall of the city. "Hezekiah cannot save you from our army! This city is going to belong to the king of Assyria. No other gods have been able to prevent us from defeating them. Don't listen to Hezekiah."

The messengers went back to the king. Hezekiah did not know what to do. He was worried. Were they going to allow the Assyrians to destroy the city and God's temple there? Then he said, "Perhaps the Lord our God has heard the words of this man when he said our God could do nothing to save us."

Hezekiah's servants then went to Isaiah and told him about the threats and insults of the enemy. Isaiah said, "Tell the king, the Lord says, 'Do not be afraid, the Lord God is going to deal with the man who speaks against Him.'"

Suddenly, there was a report that the commander's army was needed to go to another place because an attack was being made, so he could not then start his war on Jerusalem. He sent a message to Hezekiah: "Do not think you will not be defeated. I will not attack you today, but I am going to come back and destroy you. Our gods always win over the gods of our enemies."

Hezekiah took the commander's letter into the temple and prayed. He spread it out before the Lord God.

"You are the only true God of Heaven and earth and You are our God. These people have destroyed all the other nations. Now, O Lord our God, deliver us from his hand and show to all the world that You alone are God."

Then Isaiah sent a message of encouragement to Hezekiah. Isaiah reminded him that the Almighty God was with him, and he told Hezekiah that not one arrow would be shot into the city, and not one man of the enemy would enter it.

That night the angel of the Lord went out over the camp of the Assyrians, and in the morning the Assyrian king found that all his thousands of men were dead bodies. His army was destroyed. They had all died in the night. The prayers of the prophet Isaiah and the good king Hezekiah were answered.

Good kings and bad

Some of the kings who ruled over Israel and Judah were very good kings at first. But then they did things that displeased the Lord. Others were evil, and caused God's people to sin even more. One bad king was Manasseh. In time, however, he came to see the error of his ways, and this is how it happened.

When Manasseh's father, the good king Hezekiah, died, Manasseh became king. He was only twelve years old, but as he grew up he followed the shameful ways of the nations God had driven out of the land. He built altars to heathen gods; he made his son pass through fire. He practised sorcery and witchcraft, and contacted evil spirits, which God forbids, and he killed many innocent people.

God was angry and spoke to him through His servants the prophets. But neither Manasseh nor the people listened. They became worse than the other nations.

So the Lord God sent the Assyrians to attack Judah and Jerusalem. They took Manasseh and bound him in bronze shackles and carried him off to Babylon. There, Manasseh realized the evil of his ways. He repented. He prayed to God and asked to be forgiven. God listened to Manasseh, and he was released and brought back to Jerusalem. He threw out all the images and told the people to serve the Lord. He obeyed the words of God's prophets. When he died, his son Amon became king. But again he worshipped idols and so did the people.

Jeremiah was God's prophet when the next king came to the throne. He was a good king. His name was Josiah. He did that which was right in the eyes of the Lord, although he was only eight years old when he became king.

When Josiah was only twelve years of age he destroyed all the idols and their altars which had been set up in Jerusalem and Judah. He wanted to please the Lord his God.

Now the people had not been seeking God in His temple, and it was not used, nor kept properly. Josiah was eighteen years old when he gave instructions for the temple to be repaired and cleaned up. The temple was in ruins and there was a lot of work to do. Carpenters

and stonemasons were engaged to renew the timber and stonework. Then, as they were clearing out the rubbish, Hilkiah the priest found the roll of the Book of the Law of the Lord. Now no one had read God's book for years. They had forgotten that there was one! They took it to King Josiah. "Look what we have found," they said. "It is the Book of God's Law."

"Read it to me," commanded the king, and Shaphan, who was the king's secretary, read it to Josiah.

As Josiah listened to the words of the book he began to look anxious; then troubled and afraid. He said, "We have not been keeping God's word. We have not been doing what it says in this book. We shall be punished. Disaster will come upon us!" Josiah tore his royal robes in distress. "God is angry with us," he cried.

He called all the elders of Judah and Jerusalem together, and with all the people they went into the temple. There the words of the book were read out to them. When the reading was finished Josiah called on everyone to make a promise to God that they would obey His commands and words written in this book. He commanded all the people to get rid of their idols, and serve and worship the Lord only.

Josiah found in the Book of the Law that God required His people to keep the feast of the Passover every year, to remind them of how God had saved them out of Egypt. So he ordered a great and holy feast, to which everyone brought a lamb to sacrifice to the Lord. A service in the temple was arranged, and carried out as Moses had commanded the people long ago. The Passover had not been kept during the reigns of all the kings of Israel since the time of Samuel.

When Josiah died, the prophet Jeremiah wrote a song about the young king, which told of his devotion to his God, and all the good he did for God's people.

Jeremiah, the sad prophet

There were four more kings after Josiah. They were not good as he had been. They did evil in the eyes of the Lord, and the people and their leaders became more and more unfaithful to their God. They determined to worship idols and their wickedness increased year by year for forty years. God allowed the Egyptians, the Chaldeans, the Syrians, the Moabites and the Ammonites to invade the land of Judah. Then He sent Nebuchadnezzar and his armies. They partly destroyed the land and attacked Jerusalem, but still the people did not repent of their wicked ways.

For forty years Jeremiah preached to the people. God had called Jeremiah to be his prophet when he was quite young. Jeremiah said, "I am only a child." But God said, "Do not be afraid, I have chosen you to speak for Me, and I will be with you."

Jeremiah reminded the people of all the good things God had done for them. How He had saved them from being slaves in Egypt, how He had looked after them in the wilderness, and how He had given them the lovely land of Canaan. He reminded them of how He had protected them from their enemies and made them into a prosperous nation. "Now you are worshipping other gods. Why have you left the Lord, and why do you no longer walk in His ways?" Jeremiah demanded. He pleaded for them to return to their good God, and he warned them of what would happen if they refused to turn back to their Lord and Saviour. Like a good preacher, he used many examples, or parables, using familiar situations to make his message real to them. He spoke about wives who left their husbands, about the way lions and wolves destroyed people, and about the effects of good or bad harvests, and the way people were healed.

Jeremiah told the people that if they changed their ways Jerusalem would never be defeated, they would live there in peace. But if not, the city and the temple would be destroyed. Jeremiah rebuked the people, then he wept for them. He pleaded with them to give up their wicked ways and warned them of what would happen to them if they did not. He commanded them to keep the Sabbath Day holy for their

God and not to work and trade on that day. But it was all in vain, they would not give up their wicked ways. They made even more idols.

Jeremiah wore a dirty piece of cloth around his waist. When he bought this cloth it had been richly coloured and decorated, but now it looked like an old rag. This is like the nation of Judah, Jeremiah was really saying – it is fit only to be thrown away.

One day, God said, "Go down to the potter's house and see what he does." So Jeremiah went. The potter threw a lump of soft clay onto his potter's wheel and as it went round he moulded it with his hands and began to form a pot in which to carry water. But the pot was mis-shapen. So the potter squashed it all together, and started again. "That is what I will do with the nation of Judah," said God. "Judah is no good, it is like a bad pot. I will destroy it and start again, if it will not be formed the way it should be."

Another day, God told Jeremiah to go and buy a clay pot from the potter. "Take the elders outside the city and speak to them, and say to them, 'I am going to bring such a catastrophe on this city that it will make the ears of those who hear about it to tingle.' Say to them, 'Because you have forsaken Me and have worshipped other gods and have filled this place with the blood of the innocent, and because you have burned your sons in the fire as burnt offering to the god Baal, this place will be called the place of Slaughter, for your enemies will come and take away your lives. It will be terrible. Your city will be besieged by armies, you will have no food and people will be so hungry that they will be eating their own children. Then the enemy will break up the city. It will be smashed in pieces.'" As he said this Jeremiah threw down the clay pot he had in his hand and it was smashed to pieces.

Jeremiah then went to the temple and stood in the court and preached again. "The Lord of Hosts, the God of Israel, says, 'Listen, I am going to bring upon this city and on all the towns of Judah the disasters I have promised, because you have been so stubborn, and have refused to listen to My words.'"

Then Pashhur the priest, who was also chief governor in the house of the Lord, had Jeremiah beaten and put in stocks. His feet and neck and hands were fastened in a wooden frame and he was kept there. He was in pain and could not move.

It was not until the next day that the governor let him out. Jeremiah said to him, "The day of terror is coming when you will see your friends killed by the sword or taken away as captives by the enemy. They will carry off all the treasures of Jerusalem and your houses will be destroyed. You and your family will be taken off to Babylon and there you will die."

At last it happened. The people had mocked God's servants, they had not listened to His prophets and now Nebuchadnezzar laid siege to Jerusalem. His army surrounded the city.

Jeremiah again spoke to the people. "It is no good your trying to resist or stop the army. God has sent them to take you all away, as well as all the treasures of the temple."

He continued to prophesy. God showed him two baskets of figs. One was full of good figs, the other of bad figs, very bad figs. "This is what it means," God said. "The bad figs are no good, they will be thrown away. The good figs are the people whom the enemy is taking to Babylon, and whom I will keep. They and their children will come back after seventy years and will build My city again. These are those who love Me and serve Me and walk in My ways. I will be their God and will look after them."

Then the leaders threatened to kill Jeremiah. They put him in prison.

The people of Jerusalem were starving, for the enemy had prevented any food from being brought into the city for many months. Inside the city there was nothing left for them to eat. Then the army broke down the wall and set fire to the palaces and the temple of God.

When the army commander found Jeremiah in prison he released him, and did not send him away to Babylon with all the other captives. Jeremiah went to stay with some friends who were also allowed to stay in the land.

All the treasures of Judah were taken and altogether four thousand six hundred people were marched away to go to Babylon. The city of Jerusalem lay in ruins for seventy years.

Jeremiah sat outside the city wall, where Jesus was later crucified, and there he wept and wept sad tears for God's empty city, its ruined temple, and its unhappy people taken away captive. He thought about all that had happened over the past years, and then wrote a book about it, which we call 'Lamentations'.

Ezekiel's visions

Ezekiel was a prophet of God who was captured and taken away to Babylon eleven years before Jerusalem was finally destroyed.

God called Ezekiel to preach to the Israelites in their captivity. He was to remind them why they were there. Some hoped to go back home soon. But Ezekiel told them, "No, the Lord God wants to make sure you never worship idols again. You have to stay here many years."

Ezekiel told them that back in Israel, Jerusalem was going to be totally overthrown. They could not believe that it would happen to the city of God. "The sins of the people are so wicked," said Ezekiel, "that God is going to have it destroyed by Nebuchadnezzar."

God told Ezekiel to make a model of Jerusalem. He was to act out the way in which it would be besieged, and the ways in which the people would suffer.

Then, in a vision, Ezekiel saw all the wickedness of Israel in their land, and all the terrible suffering they were to endure in Jerusalem.

Eventually, news arrived that the city had fallen and later, the captured Israelites arrived in Babylon.

Later on, Ezekiel began to tell the people in captivity of the days when they would go back again to the land, having learned their lesson. He told them of a day coming when all God's people would form a living nation by the Spirit of God. He told them of One to come who would be a King over all His people, from all over the world. Ezekiel was shown a vision of the true temple of God in God's city – and of a river which would go out from it for the healing of the nations. The name of the city was to be, 'The Lord is there.'

Daniel and the king's dream

Among those who were taken away captive to Babylon was a lively young man named Daniel.

The king, Nebuchadnezzar, ordered that the best looking and the most intelligent young men should be set aside from among the captives for special training. So the most handsome youths who were also quick to learn were taught the ways of the Babylonians. They were to be trained for three years in the language and learning of that nation. They were to have the best food, and then they were to enter the king's service. Among those who were chosen was Daniel, and three of his friends.

One day, Daniel and his friends said to the officer, "We cannot eat this rich food and drink this red wine. Give us plain food and vegetables to eat, and water to drink."

"I cannot do that," the officer replied, "you will not look well and healthy unless you eat our food and drink our wine."

"Try my way for ten days," Daniel said, "and see how we look then."

The officer agreed, and at the end of the ten days Daniel and his three friends looked fresher and healthier than all the other men.

The officer brought them before King Nebuchadnezzar who was very pleased with them. He found that they were ten times wiser and understood more than all the other wise men in his kingdom.

One night, King Nebuchadnezzar had dreams which frightened him. He was very disturbed. So he called his magicians, sorcerers, enchanters and astrologers. "I have had a fearful dream," he said. "It must mean something. Tell me the meaning."

"O King, live forever," they said. "Tell us your dream and we will tell you what it means."

"If you are as clever as you are supposed to be, you will tell me the dream, as well as its meaning."

"Sir," they replied, "no one can do that."

Nebuchadnezzar was afraid, and very angry. "Put all my wise men to death," he cried. Now Daniel and his friends were not there, but when they found out about the king's decree Daniel wanted to know why he, and all the wise men, were to be killed. So they told him. Daniel went to the king and told him that if he would spare their lives he would come back to the king the next day after he had prayed to the Lord. Then he went back to his friends and urged them to pray to God that their lives might be spared.

That night the Lord revealed the mystery in a vision to Daniel. Then Daniel praised the God of Heaven, and next morning he went to Arioch, the man who was to execute the magicians. "Take me to the king," said Daniel, "I will explain his majesty's dream to him."

"Are you able to tell me what I saw, and are you able to tell me what it means?" demanded King Nebuchadnezzar.

"Your wise men cannot explain this mysterious dream to you, but there is a God in Heaven who can, and He has revealed it to your servant," replied Daniel.

"O King, you saw a vision in the night. As you watched you saw a tremendous statue. It was enormous; it stood there in shining brightness and almost took your breath away.

"As you looked, you saw that its head was of pure gold, its chest and arms were of silver, its belly and thighs were bronze, it had legs of iron, and its feet were partly of iron and partly of baked clay.

"As you were watching you saw a stone was being cut out. This stone struck the great image on its feet and smashed them to pieces. Then the great image came crashing down to the ground, dissolving into dust. The wind came and blew it all away. Nothing remained, except the stone that struck the image. Then, it began to grow and grow, becoming a great mountain which filled the whole earth.

"This was your dream, O King, and this is the meaning of it. God has given you power and made you into a great kingdom. You are that head of gold. After you shall rise another kingdom to rule the world, not so glorious as yours. Then, a third kingdom shall come. The fourth kingdom will not be so strong and will be partly iron and partly baked clay.

"In the days of those kings, the God of Heaven will set up a kingdom and it will fill the whole world. It will never be destroyed."

Nebuchadnezzar was so pleased with Daniel for telling him the meaning of the dream that he made Daniel ruler over the whole province of Babylon. He was also put in charge of all the other wise men. The king gave Daniel many gifts and honours. "The great God has shown me what He is going to do," he said, "and He has told me about His kingdom which is to come." And Nebuchadnezzar praised the great God of Heaven.

The burning fiery furnace

Time went on and the king forgot about the true God. And then King Nebuchadnezzar had an idea. "I will make a great golden image ninety-nine feet high." (This would be nearly four times as high as an ordinary house.) "I will set it up in the plain of Dura where everyone can come and see it. They will come from all the countries I have conquered and when the music plays all the people will fall down and worship the great golden image I have set up."

So the people and officials came from all the lands across the sea to worship Nebuchadnezzar's golden image.

But the three friends of Daniel (called Shadrach, Meshach and Abednego) refused to bow down because they knew that there was only one God to whom they should bow. He made the heavens and the earth. They were not going to worship any image, however grand it was.

"Did you not say, O king," said some of Nebuchadnezzar's wise men, "did you not say that if anyone does not bow down and worship your image they would be thrown into the burning fiery furnace?"

"Indeed I did," affirmed the king. "Who dares to disobey my orders?"

"When the music starts to play there are some Jews who do not bow down to your image, O king."

"Send them to me!" roared King Nebuchadnezzar.

"Is it true," he demanded of Shadrach, Meshach and Abednego, "that when you hear the music you do not worship and bow down to the golden image I have set up? Next time you hear this music, you bow down to my image, and all will be well with you. But, if you do not – you will be straightway thrown into the burning fiery furnace. Then we shall see if there is a God who can rescue you from my hands!"

Then answered Shadrach, Meshach and Abednego: "O king, we cannot bow down to your gods, nor to the image you have set up. We worship the God of Heaven. If you throw us into the furnace, our God whom we serve will deliver us; but even if He does not save us, we will not bow down to the image of gold you have set up."

Nebuchadnezzar went into a rage. "Heat up the furnace seven times hotter than usual. Tie them up and throw them into the burning fire!"

Some of his mighty men then tied up the three friends, bundled them to the entrance of the furnace, still wearing their coats and turbans and threw them into the roaring flames. So hot was the furnace that the soldiers who threw them in were killed by the intense heat. The three brave men fell down in the blazing furnace of fire as Nebuchadnezzar and all his officers watched.

As the king looked, he stared in amazement. What did he see? Turning to his officials, he asked, "Was it not three men we tied up and threw into the fire?" They answered, "True, O king."

"But I can plainly see four men, their binding ropes are untied, and they are walking about in the fire unharmed, and the fourth one is like a son of the gods."

Nebuchadnezzar jumped up and came as near as he dared to the entrance of the furnace. He stared in disbelief. How could this happen? The three young men had told him that God could save them from the flames and it looked very much as if their God was able to deliver them. What could he do now? He called to them, "Shadrach, Meshach and Abednego, servants of the Most High God, come out of the flames, and come here!"

Then everyone saw the three friends walk out of the fire. The people were astonished as they saw that they were not burnt, their clothes were not singed, nor was there any smell of fire on them.

Nebuchadnezzar and all his governors and officials who were watching crowded around to see if there was any sign of burning on these three young men. They saw that not one hair of their heads was singed, and none of their clothes was burnt or even smelt of smoke.

Then the king made a decree. He said, "Blessed be the God of Shadrach, Meshach and Abednego, who sent His angel and delivered His servants who trusted in Him. They were ready to die, rather than serve or worship any god except their God.

"Therefore, I make a decree that no one is to speak against the God of Shadrach, Meshach and Abednego, because there is no other God who can deliver like this."

So the three friends were promoted to high positions in the province. They continued faithful to God in the land of the Babylonians.

The den of lions

Nebuchadnezzar, the great king over all the nations, had another dream which none of his wise men could understand, except Daniel. He dreamt about a tremendous tree and that it was cut down by the orders of a holy one from Heaven.

"That tree is you, O king," Daniel told him. "But if you humble yourself before God and ask Him to forgive all the wrong things you have done, it may be that the Lord God will continue to let you be king."

A year later, as the king was starting to boast about all he had done and what a great king he was, suddenly the Lord God made him to become like an animal. He was not able to be king, but was like a mad man for seven years. After that, God healed him and he sat on his throne again, and became an even greater king than he had been before. He wrote a letter to the people of all his dominions, telling them all that the Most High God had done for him, and he praised and honoured the Lord God Who had made him a king. After that, Nebuchadnezzar lived a life which was pleasing to God, until he died.

Then, Belshazzar became king, but he did not reverence the Lord God as Nebuchadnezzar had done, nor did he count Daniel as one of his wise men. One day he made a great feast for all his nobles. He used the holy golden cups which had been brought from the Lord's house in Jerusalem. Then he praised the gods of gold and silver, bronze and iron and wood. As Belshazzar was drinking wine and praising all his idol gods a frightening thing happened. A hand appeared writing all by itself on the wall. The laughing and joking of the banquet suddenly stopped. "Call my wise men and see what it means!" the king cried.

They came, but none could tell him. The king's face became deadly white. What could it mean?

The queen reminded Belshazzar that in Nebuchadnezzar's day Daniel had been his adviser. "Call Daniel," she said.

So Daniel came. "I have heard that you are intelligent and can solve difficult problems. I will put a gold chain around your neck and make you third ruler in the land if you can tell me what that writing on the wall means," said Belshazzar.

"You may keep your gifts," Daniel replied. "You knew that the Most High God blessed your ancestor. You knew that Nebuchadnezzar found out that the God of Heaven raises up kings and rules over all this world, and now you are praising other gods and drinking out of the holy golden cups from the temple of God. You have not honoured the God of Glory. The meaning of the words are these: 'Your reign as king is finished. You have not lived in a way pleasing to God, and your kingdom is given to the Medes and Persians.'"

That very night, Darius the Mede came, the kingdom was overthrown, and Belshazzar was killed.

Darius was king now, and Daniel became one of the three most important men in the king's court. Darius the Great found Daniel to be the wisest man in his kingdom, and planned to set him over all the other rulers in the land. Daniel would be the most powerful man under the king.

The other wise men did not like this. They were jealous. Daniel was a Jew, he came from another land. They tried to find out how they could get him into trouble. But Daniel did his work well. He was honest, he never broke any of the laws, he did not do anything wrong. He served the king faithfully and well.

"We must find some way to get rid of him," those wicked men said. Then they thought of an idea. "We know that he prays faithfully to his God," they said. "That is how we can catch him out." So they went to the king.

"O King Darius, live for ever! All your royal advisers have agreed that you should make a law. We have thought it would be good and right for you to make a law which says that if anyone should pray to any god or man, except you, O king, for thirty days, they shall be thrown into the lions' den. We must know that all your people are faithful to you. Now, we must get the law written and sealed and signed, for then it cannot be changed or altered."

So the law was written and sealed by the king.

When Daniel heard that the law had been made he knew that he would not stop praying to the Lord Who loved him. He went home to his house, and where his windows opened toward Jerusalem, he knelt down and prayed to the Lord God three times every day as he had always done. He thanked God for His goodness to him. He prayed that God would forgive his sins and the sins of his people, and he asked God that they might go home again one day to their own land and serve Him there.

The wise men were watching. They then ran to the king. "Did you not make a law which says that anyone who asks or prays to any god or person, except to you, O king, shall be thrown in the lions' den?"

"That is so," said Darius, "and the laws of the Medes and Persians cannot be changed."

"We have found someone who pays no attention to you, O king, nor to your law! It is Daniel. He prays three times every day to His god."

Now the king loved Daniel. He was very sad when he realized what had happened, and he tried to think of ways in which to save Daniel. He was his best and most trusted servant.

"Remember, O king," those wicked men said, "the laws of the

Medes and the Persians cannot be changed. You signed the law."

What could the king do? He could find no way to save Daniel his good servant. Daniel had to be thrown to the hungry lions. King Darius spoke to his friend Daniel. "May your God, Whom you serve all the time, may He save you!" he said in his distress.

Then they took Daniel to the den where they kept the lions, pushed him in, and rolled the stone back into place, fastening it securely.

King Darius could not eat his supper that night. Nor did he want any music to be played. When he went to bed he could get no sleep for thinking about his good and faithful servant Daniel. He tossed and turned all night long.

As soon as it was light, he rose and hurried to the lions' den. "Daniel!" he cried when he arrived. "Has your God Whom you serve been able to save you from the lions?"

Then came a voice from the den: "O king, live for ever! My God sent His angel to shut the lions' mouths. They have not hurt me because I have done nothing wrong in His sight, nor have I done any wrong to you, O king."

How happy Darius was! "Lift Daniel out of the den," he ordered. When Daniel was brought out there was not a scratch or bite to be found on him anywhere.

By order of the king those wicked men who had accused Daniel and had him thrown to the lions were taken and thrown into the den themselves. The lions immediately jumped upon them and tore them to pieces. The lions, who did not want their supper, soon ate up their breakfast.

Then King Darius wrote to all the nations and people of every language.

"Peace be to you. I am writing to you to tell you to reverence and serve the God of Daniel. He is the living God. His kingdom shall never be overthrown. He has saved Daniel from the lions. All my people should worship the Lord God."

So Daniel served the Lord his God and ruled in the empire under Darius the king.

Going home

The next emperor of Persia after Darius was Cyrus, and Daniel served him also. Cyrus ruled in Babylon and was moved in his heart by the Lord God to make a proclamation and send it out to all his provinces. This is what it said:

"By order of Cyrus, king of Persia: The Eternal God of Heaven has given me all the kingdoms of the earth, and He has appointed me to see that His temple is built again in Jerusalem. All the Jews throughout my kingdom may now return and build the temple of the God of Israel."

The Lord God had allowed His people to be captured and taken away from their land because of their sins. Now, after many years, they could go back to their land again. Jeremiah had made a prophecy a long while before this that the Jews would be in captivity for seventy years. Three times the prophet Isaiah had even told the people the name of the king who would send them back again. It was to be Cyrus. The time had now come.

Cyrus helped all the people who wanted to return to their land. He gave them all the golden bowls and cups which Nebuchadnezzar had taken from the temple long ago. Besides that, he gave them over five thousand articles of gold and silver and everything else they needed for the journey.

He gave them horses and mules and camels, and more than six thousand donkeys to carry everything for them. He also sent one of his officers to look after them. The Jews who stayed behind helped their friends who were going. More than fifty thousand people collected together for the march back. The journey took them many weeks. Most of them were from the tribe of Judah, but some came from the other tribes of Israel.

When at last they arrived at Jerusalem, the first thing their leaders did was to build an altar and sacrifice to the Lord Who had brought them back again.

Then they began the work. The rubble had to be cleared away. Great stones had to be shaped and laid in place. Trees had to be cut

down. When the people saw the temple beginning to be built up, they praised God with great thanksgiving and rejoicing. The priests blew the trumpets and everyone was glad. Some of the older people, who remembered the old temple, cried, and looked forward to the day when it would be finished.

The work took a long time. At last the temple was built, and they held their first service. It was the Passover, which reminded the people of how God had saved them long ago and brought them out of Egypt. They also thanked God that He had made the king willing to let them come back and build.

More people came from Babylon with more help from a new king, Artaxerxes. With them was a man called Ezra. He was a priest and a teacher of God's law, and he taught the people from God's book. He was anxious that they would not sin again against their God, and never again did they worship heathen idols. They had learned their lesson.

At this time, although the temple was built, the wall around the city was still in ruins. The Jews were open to attack from their enemies, who did not want them to build the wall and defend themselves. Life was hard for the people, they were poor, and they were discouraged. At any time the enemies around them could come in and plunder their property.

One man who had stayed behind in Babylon was Nehemiah. He served King Artaxerxes in his palace.

Nehemiah's brother had come back from Jerusalem and told Nehemiah about the state of Jerusalem and the poor people there. "They are in great trouble. There is no one in charge, the wall is broken down, and the raiding parties keep stealing their goods and their food."

It made Nehemiah very sad to hear this. He mourned for God's people in Jerusalem for several days, and he ate nothing at all. Then he prayed before the God of Heaven. (Nehemiah was a great man of prayer.) He said, "I pray You, the Lord God of Heaven, O great and awesome God. You are merciful and keep Your promises with those who love You and obey Your commands; please listen to me and hear my prayer, and see how I am praying to You day and night. I am praying for Your people and I am confessing their sins which they have sinned against You. I and my family have sinned also. We have not obeyed the commandments which You gave to Your servant Moses. You have said to Your people, 'If you are unfaithful to Me and sin, I will scatter you among the nations', and that is what You have done, O Lord. But You have also said, 'If you return to Me and keep My commandments, I will gather you together again and you will dwell in the place I have chosen for you.'

"We are sorry for what we have done, and You did promise to bring Your people back to the land and to the city of Jerusalem. But Your people are in great distress there. The walls and gates of the city are still broken down. Can You not help Your people now?"

The next day, Nehemiah was serving King Artaxerxes with his drink, when the king said, "What is the matter with you, Nehemiah? Why are you looking so sad? You are not ill, so what is wrong with you?"

Nehemiah prayed for God to help him say the right thing. "May the king live for ever!" he said. "Why should I not be sad? The city of Jerusalem is in ruins, and my people are in trouble there."

"What do you want me to do?" asked the king.

Then Nehemiah was very bold. He said, "Send me to Judah to get the walls of the city built up again. May I have letters from you for permission to get timber from the forests to build the gates?"

The king agreed to Nehemiah's requests and he gave Nehemiah a band of soldiers to protect him, as well.

When Nehemiah arrived he found that no one was doing anything about building a wall. So he went out one night with a few men to see what needed doing.

Next day, he called the priests, nobles and officials together and told them why he had come. Then he said, "Let us rebuild the wall of Jerusalem." He told them how God had put it into the heart of the king to let him come.

"Let us start!" he said. So they set to work.

When their enemies heard that they had begun to build the wall they were angry and tried every way to stop the work. But every man worked with a will, and each carried a sword on his belt, or had his spear beside him. If the trumpet blew, then they all left their work and gathered to the trumpet to fight off any attack.

The walls rose up. The great gates were built with strong bolts and bars, and before long the city was safe once more. The wall was finished. Then the people came to a great day of dedication and thanksgiving, with joy and with music.

Nehemiah organized the people. He saw to it that right was done to all, and that God's law was kept as it should be.

In everything he did Nehemiah prayed to God, and God helped him to do the work which needed to be done.

Now they were back in their land and waiting for the Messiah Who the prophets had said would be coming.

The New Testament

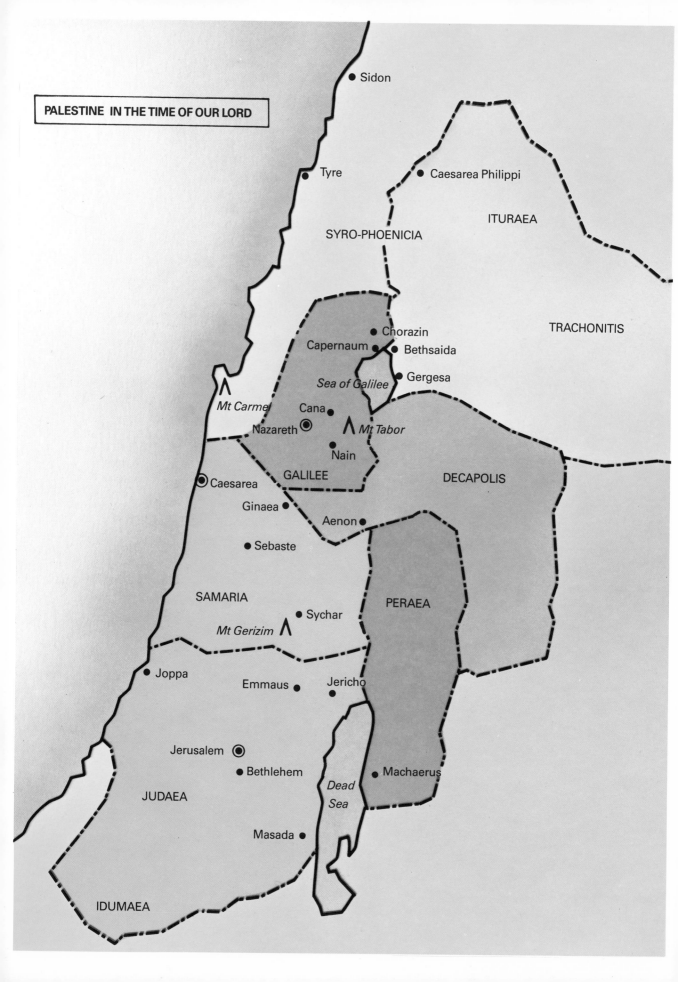

PALESTINE IN THE TIME OF OUR LORD

Sidon

Tyre

Caesarea Philippi

SYRO-PHOENICIA

ITURAEA

TRACHONITIS

Chorazin

Capernaum

Bethsaida

Gergesa

Sea of Galilee

Mt Carmel

Cana

Mt Tabor

Nazareth

Nain

Caesarea

GALILEE

DECAPOLIS

Ginaea

Aenon

Sebaste

SAMARIA

PERAEA

Mt Gerizim

Sychar

Joppa

Emmaus

Jericho

Jerusalem

Bethlehem

Machaerus

Dead Sea

JUDAEA

Masada

IDUMAEA

God's kingdom is coming

We have come to the end of the stories of the Old Testament. In the beginning everything was perfect in the wonderful world which God had made. Adam and Eve and all the animals were happy together until the first man and woman began to distrust and then disobey the Lord God. We remember that God promised to send a deliverer to overcome the evil one and save His own people. God showed His people that it was to be by sacrifice, just as long ago Abel sacrificed a lamb, which died for his sins. All God's people made the same sacrifice until the day when God's Lamb of Sacrifice should come. Noah worshipped God with a sacrifice when he was saved from the great flood. Abraham, Isaac and Jacob sacrificed animals on their altars to God for their sins. The Children of Israel sacrificed a lamb on the night when God delivered them out of their slavery in Egypt. Moses taught the people how to worship God by sacrifice at the tabernacle, or worship tent. They did the same when they came to the land promised to them by the Lord God. There they built the temple with its Altar of Sacrifice.

God had promised that the Saviour would come from the tribe of Judah. The prophet Micah said He would be born in Bethlehem. The prophets wrote of the kind of Person He would be, and what He would do. They said He would be betrayed and that He would suffer for His people's sins. They told just how He would die and be buried. David, in the Psalms, spoke of His rising up from the dead and being received into Heaven to be king over all who love Him.

Four great world empires had risen. We have read of the Assyrian empire, which rose to power and came to an end. The mighty Persian empire followed. Then came the Greek empire. This was followed by the Roman empire. Daniel the prophet spoke of these coming empires and he said that in the days of this last world empire the God of Heaven would set up His eternal kingdom.

As we begin the New Testament we find that the Roman army has occupied the land of Israel (now called Palestine), and that Herod, a cruel king, has been put in charge of the nation.

Angels appear

For many years now there had been no prophet of God speaking to the people of Israel. The prophets of old had said that a Saviour would come. For a long while, God had not spoken to His people. Since those long ago days, the Romans had come, and the land of Judaea was now ruled by them. They had made Herod king, and Roman soldiers kept order in the land. The Jews were allowed to worship in the way they had always done.

Zechariah was a priest. He and his wife Elizabeth were godly people who were careful to obey God's laws. They lived to please Him. This man and his wife had been married for many years, but they had no children.

It was now the turn of Zechariah to go to the temple in Jerusalem to offer incense on the golden altar in God's presence. While all the people were outside praying, Zechariah was startled. He saw the angel of the Lord standing by the altar. He stood back, gripped with fear.

"Do not be afraid, Zechariah, your prayers have been heard. You will have a son, and you will call his name John. He will be devoted to God, and will not drink wine, nor any other strong drink. He will be a mighty prophet of God, like Elijah. He will preach to the people and prepare them for the coming of the Lord."

This was tremendous news. Zechariah could hardly believe his ears. He said to the angel, "How can this be? I am getting old now, and so is Elizabeth my wife. We cannot expect to have a baby at our time of life."

The angel replied, "I am Gabriel. I stand in the presence of God. I have been sent to speak to you and tell you this good news. You will not now be able to speak until the day arrives, because you did not believe my words."

All the people were waiting outside, wondering why Zechariah was taking such a long time that day. When he came out he could not speak, but made signs to them until they realized that he had seen a vision in the temple of God, and could not say anything.

Six months later, the angel Gabriel came to earth again. This time he went to a young girl in the little town of Nazareth. Her name was Mary. She was engaged to be married to a young man by the name of Joseph.

"Greetings to you! The Lord is with you and has highly favoured you."

Mary was astonished. Whatever could this mean? What was happening?

"Do not be afraid, Mary. You are to have a son, and you are to give him the name Jesus. He will be great, and will be called the Son of the Most High. He is the One promised to King David, and His kingdom will be greater than King David's – for it will be for ever."

"How could this ever be?" Mary exclaimed in amazement. "I am not even married!"

"The Holy Spirit will come upon you, and the power of the Most High will cover you, and the Holy One to be born to you will be called the Son of God."

Then, the angel told Mary that Elizabeth, who was a relative of hers, was also going to have a son; and Mary believed all he said.

She said, "I am the Lord's servant. Let it be as you have said."

The angel left her and went away.

Mary was excited. Whom could she tell? Who would understand? Why – Elizabeth would! She made herself ready and hurried away to the hill country, to the village where Zechariah and Elizabeth lived.

"Come in!" called Elizabeth. "How glad I am to see you! My baby jumped inside me when he heard your voice at the door. God has blessed you. You are going to have a child, too. I know He is to be our Lord, because I felt my baby move for joy inside me. You believed that God would do what He said, and you are blessed."

Then, Mary sang a wonderful song of praise to the Lord, which begins:

'My soul magnifies the Lord,
And my spirit rejoices in God my Saviour.'

So Mary stayed with Elizabeth for three months and then went back to her home.

In due time, Elizabeth's baby was born. Just as he was being named John, to everyone's astonishment Zechariah's voice came back. He was filled with the Holy Spirit and spoke some wonderful words about baby John.

Zechariah told the people, "John is going to be God's prophet to turn the people away from their sins and prepare them for the coming of the Lord Jesus. We are living in marvellous days."

How Jesus came

Now there lived in the city of Nazareth a fine young man by the name of Joseph. Joseph came to know and love a very sweet girl who loved the Lord God. Her name was Mary. They became engaged to be married. Then something happened which greatly distressed Joseph. Before they were married he found out – perhaps Mary told him – that she was going to have a baby. How could this be? Surely, his dear Mary had not been unfaithful to him and gone with some other man?

Joseph did not know what to do. Should he not now get married to Mary if she had been with some other man? He could not sleep that night for thinking about it. He was hurt in his heart. When at last he did get to sleep an angel of the Lord appeared to him in a dream. The angel said, "Joseph, you who come from the royal family of King David, do not be afraid to take Mary to be your wife. The baby that is coming is not coming because Mary has been with any other man. The baby is coming because of the working of God the Holy Spirit in her body. The baby is going to be a boy, and you will call His name Jesus, for He is going to save His people from their sins."

This was tremendous news. God Himself was the Father of Mary's baby. How wonderful! When he awoke Joseph hurried to see Mary and tell her about the words of the angel. Then they were married.

Mary's baby inside her body grew larger every day, until it was almost time for Him to be born. It was then that Augustus Caesar, the Emperor in Rome, made a decree which said that everyone in all the countries over which he ruled must be registered, so that they could be taxed.

Mary and Joseph had to make the long journey to Bethlehem to be registered there. Now, Bethlehem, called David's City, was nearly seventy miles away over rough hilly roads, and it would take them several days' travelling to reach the little town. You can imagine that poor Mary was anxious about that kind of a journey when she was expecting her precious baby to be born. But they had to go. Joseph tried to make it as easy as he could for his young wife.

At last they arrived, tired and dusty, only to find that the town was full up with people who had come to register their names also. What were they to do? Where could they stay? Where could Joseph find a bed, or a room for his dear wife to rest? Their baby was about to be born.

At last, he found a stable where animals were kept, and there, that very night, Jesus was born. They had no clean bed for themselves, nor pretty cot for the baby Jesus. Joseph did his best to make a bed for the baby in a manger. This was a kind of box from which the animals fed. Jesus was wrapped up warmly in pieces of cloth, and this is how the Saviour of the world was born. The Son of God had arrived, and no one knew, except Mary and Joseph.

But, wait – there were others who knew, and they were even now coming to look for, and find, the One born to be King.

In the fields outside Bethlehem were shepherds looking after their flocks through the night. Without warning, a strange light appeared, and a glory began to shine all around them. The shepherds were frightened. Then, the voice of an angel announced: "Do not be afraid. I bring you good tidings of great joy, which is for all people. For to you, this very day, has been born in David's City, a Saviour. He is Christ the Lord. You will find Him wrapped in swaddling bands, lying in a manger."

When the angel had said this, suddenly a great number of other angels appeared, all praising God, and saying:

> 'Glory to God in high Heaven,
> And peace on earth;
> Good will from God to men.'

After a while, they went away again to Heaven, and all was quiet.

The shepherds began to talk to one another. "What are we waiting for?" they said. "Let's go to Bethlehem and see this thing which has happened, about which the Lord has told us."

So they hurried off to the town and discovered Mary and Joseph and the baby. He was wrapped in swaddling bands and was lying in a manger, just as they had been told.

Mary and Joseph were surprised that the shepherd men should come and see them and their new baby. The shepherds told everyone they met about the angels, and what they had said about this baby. All who heard it wondered what it could mean, but Mary especially kept these wonderful things in her heart. The shepherds went back to their flocks praising God and glorifying Him.

Joseph and Mary stayed in Bethlehem for a while. They were not many miles from the temple in Jerusalem. As soon as they were able, they took their baby to the temple to offer a sacrifice and to present Him to the Lord God. He was named Jesus, which means, Saviour. This is what the angel had told Joseph, because Jesus was to be the One who would save His people from their sins.

While they were in the temple two things happened. First, a man called Simeon came in. Simeon was a devout man of God. He lived in the presence of God, and he knew by the Holy Spirit of God that he would not die before he had seen the One Whom the Lord had promised to send to His people. He came into the temple just at the time when Mary and Joseph and the baby Jesus were there. When Simeon saw them he knew that this baby was the One he had been waiting to see. He took Him in his arms and blessed and praised God:

'Lord God, my eyes have now seen Your salvation,
Which is for all the people of the world.
I am glad, for now I can die in peace,
For You have done that which You promised to Your people.'

Mary and Joseph stood there amazed at what Simeon was saying about the little baby Jesus. But then, Simeon had something else to say:

"Listen, Mary. For some, this Child shall be their downfall, but many shall be blessed and lifted up by Him. He will show people what is in their hearts, and they will be against Him. Your own heart will also be sad."

At that moment, a very old lady came in, and she too saw the baby Jesus. She loved God, and was always in the temple, going without her food and spending her time in prayer. She was a prophetess, and her name was Anna. When she saw Jesus she also thanked God and praised the Lord. Then, she told all the people who had been expecting the Saviour to come, that this was the One for Whom they waited.

Mary and Joseph did not know what to think about all these happenings, as they returned to the place where they were staying with the baby God had given them.

Wise men arrive

While Jesus was still very young, strangers arrived in Jerusalem. They were wise men from the east. For years they had studied the stars in the night sky, and the way in which they appeared to move in order across the heavens. There came a day when they were mystified by the appearance of a new star. It was different from all the other lights they had ever seen. Compared with other stars, it was near. It seemed to hang over the land toward the west. A great king must have been born there, they said, and so they followed the star until they came to the land of Judaea.

The wise men made their way to the chief city, for they thought, "That is where the king will be found."

They asked in Jerusalem, "Where is he that is born King of the Jews? For we have seen his star from our country, and we have followed it here. We know that someone very great has been born, and we are come to worship him."

When King Herod heard that wise men from the east had come to worship a new king, he was not at all happy. In fact, he was very worried – for was he not the king? Who, then, was this new Child? He did not want someone else coming to be king, and taking his throne.

He hurriedly called the priests and the teachers of the Holy Scriptures to assemble before him.

"You say that the Messiah, the Christ, is to come?"

"Yes," they said.

"Where is He going to be born?" Herod wanted to know.

They answered him: "The prophet in the scripture tells us that it will be in Bethlehem." And they read out to him the words of the prophet Micah:

"But you, Bethlehem, in the land of Judah,
Are not the least among the rulers of Judah;
For out of you shall come a Ruler
Who will be the shepherd of My people Israel."

Herod sent the chief priests and scribes away. He then called in the wise men who had come so far to see the new King, and told them, "If there is a person born to be king you will find him in Bethlehem. Search for him carefully, and when you have found him, come back and tell me, for I want to worship him, too."

They did not find it very difficult, because as soon as they started to go to Bethlehem there was the star they had seen before. They were so glad to see it again. It led them on until it stopped right over the house where the young Child was. When they went into the house, there was the One they had come to see, with His mother Mary at his side.

What a surprise for Mary and Joseph! When these important persons saw the little Jesus they bowed down and worshipped Him! Before they left, the visitors opened the gifts they had brought with them. Mary could hardly believe her eyes. There was real gold, expensive and sweet smelling incense, as well as myrrh which cost a great deal. They were gifts for a king!

That night, the wise men were warned by God in a dream not to go back to King Herod. He did not want to worship Jesus Christ at all — he wanted to kill Him! So they returned to their own country by another way.

The angel of the Lord also came to Joseph in a dream.

"Get up!" he said. "Take the child now and hurry away to Egypt. King Herod is coming to search for the little One, in order to kill Him."

Joseph got up straightaway and they left that night, as the angel had told him.

When the wise men did not come back to King Herod, that wicked man ordered that all the baby boys of up to two years old should be killed, thinking that Jesus would certainly be destroyed also. But Joseph and Mary were safely on their way.

It was not long before King Herod died. The angel came to Joseph in Egypt, and told him in a dream to go back again to Israel. Joseph did as the angel said, and made the journey back to his own land with Jesus and Mary his wife. They went back to live in their own town of Nazareth in Galilee.

Jesus goes to the temple

Joseph and Mary watched Jesus as He grew. Soon, He was able to walk and then to run about. He learned to talk and play and help His mother. Jesus was like all the other children, but there was something different about Him. No one ever saw Him in a bad mood, or grumpy. He never seemed to boast, or quarrel, or fight, or tell lies. Nor did He do silly things. He did what He was asked to do quite happily. He loved best to hear the Old Testament stories His mother told Him about what God had done in days gone by. He learned to read about Abraham, Moses and King David. He read the Psalms and what the prophets said.

Every year, Joseph and Mary made the journey to Jerusalem to keep the Passover Feast. When they came back, Jesus wanted to know all about the priests and their garments, and the worship and sacrifices in the temple in Jerusalem. He looked forward to the time when He could go to the House of God and hear the teachers explaining God's Word. When He was twelve years old it was time for Him to make the trip.

The services lasted a whole week. Each family, or family group, brought a lamb to the temple. There, it had to be killed and it was then taken to the people's home, or wherever they were staying. The lamb was cooked, and as the families ate it, they remembered how God had brought them out of Egypt to the land of promise.

For the first time, the boy Jesus attended the solemn services of the temple and ate the Passover with His family and friends. While others went around the markets and shops, what Jesus most liked to do was to hear the Word of God read and explained by the teachers. The week soon passed. His family prepared to leave for home. Joseph and Mary thought that Jesus was coming along with their friends. But, at the end of the first day's journey, when they looked for Him among the people, He was not to be found. They were worried. Where was He? No one had seen Him. Was He lost? The next day, instead of going on home, they travelled all the way back to Jerusalem. It was not until the following day that they found Him.

And where do you think He was? Why, in the temple, sitting with the teachers, listening to them and asking questions! Everyone was amazed at His understanding of God and His Word.

But His mother was cross. "What are You doing? Why were You not with us? We have been searching for You everywhere."

"Didn't you know where to look for Me?" Jesus asked. "Didn't you realize that I would be in My Father's house?"

Jesus got up and went with them to Nazareth. There He honoured His parents and did what they said. Joseph taught Jesus how to make many fine things from wood. So, Jesus grew up to be a man, working in the carpenter's work-shop. Everyone noticed how gracious and wise He was. In every way, the blessing of God was upon Him.

Jesus is baptized

When the people attended the services at the synagogue or the temple in Jerusalem they listened to the teachers of the law. But they often spoke in a very boring way. It did not seem very exciting. Then one day, people began to talk about a man who was not teaching the people in the synagogues. He was preaching out in the country near the river Jordan. He did not talk like the priests. He had a commanding voice, and what he had to say made everyone listen. All the people went out to hear his preaching. They had never heard anything like it.

The preacher's name was John, the cousin of Jesus, and he was called John the Baptist because he baptized people in the river Jordan. John was not dressed in priestly robes. He wore clothes made out of rough camel's hair with a leather belt around his waist. Neither did he go to the market to buy the best foods, but he ate what he could find in the country – locusts and wild honey.

But it was his preaching that people came to hear! They said, "This is a true prophet of God – he must be a greater preacher than Elijah of old. God is speaking to His people again."

John the Baptist had a startling announcement to make: "The kingdom of Heaven is at hand! Repent of your sins and be ready – the kingdom of Heaven is about to come."

Now, this is what the prophet Isaiah had said in his prophecy long ago. These are his words:

"There will be the voice of one crying in the wilderness,
'Prepare the way of the Lord, make ready His paths.'"

There was great excitement and many wondered what was going to happen. Everyone went out to hear John preaching in the wilderness. John said, "I am telling you that there is One coming Who is greater than me. I baptize you with water, He is going to baptize you with the Holy Spirit. Get ready for Him. He is coming."

When John preached, many people came to realize that God was not pleased with the way they lived, and that unless they did something about it, God would punish them. John was not afraid to preach to the priests and teachers who came to see him and hear him. "You are sinners, too," he cried. "God will cut you down like a fruit tree which grows no fruit. Repent of all your sins, and bring forth good fruit. Be kind, and not cruel. You are greedy and you don't really love God at all. Repent of all your selfish ways and be baptized in this river Jordan, or you will be in danger from the judgment of God!"

Many people listened to John. They knew he was right, they wanted to be rid of all their sins, and they were baptized in the Jordan river.

Then, one day as John was preaching to the people, he saw Someone coming to him. It was Jesus. "This is the One," he cried. "He is the Lamb of God Who has come to take away the sins of the world! I am not good enough even to be His servant."

Jesus came to John and asked to be baptized.

"No," said John, "You do not need to be baptized. You ought to be baptizing me!"

"I want you to baptize Me," said Jesus.

So Jesus went down into the Jordan. As He came up out of the water the heavens above opened, and the Spirit of God came like a dove and settled on Him. Then, a voice from Heaven was heard: "This is My Son, Whom I love. I am well pleased with Him."

Jesus was about thirty years old. Straightaway after this, he went into the desert places to prepare Himself for what He had come to do. He needed to be alone with God, to think and to pray. The Spirit of God led Him into the wilderness where He was among the wild animals. For days He wandered in the waste places, without having anything to eat. It was then that the devil, God's enemy, came to tempt Jesus to do wrong. The tempter said to Jesus, "If You were the Son of God, You would only have to tell these stones to become bread, and it would happen."

Jesus was hungry. He knew that He had the power to do this if He so chose. But He was not going to do for Himself what other people could not do when they were hungry. No, He would not do this just for Himself. Jesus replied, "It is written in the Scripture, 'Man does not live by bread alone, he needs every word which comes from the mouth of God.'" He meant that there were more important things than feeding our bodies. People have a deep need in their hearts which only God's Word to them will satisfy.

Next, the devil took Him to the highest point of the temple. "Show the people what You can do; throw Yourself down; God will send His angels to catch You and prevent You from hurting Yourself."

But Jesus did not come to make a show. He was not going to make everyone believe in Him by that kind of demonstration. "Do not tempt the Lord your God," He said to Satan.

Then, the devil took Him to a very high mountain and showed Him all the mighty kingdoms of the world. "I will give You them all if You will bow down and worship me," said Satan.

"Oh no!" said Jesus. "Get away from Me, Satan! It is written, 'You shall worship the Lord your God and Him only shall you serve.'"

Then, Satan left Him for that time. Jesus felt weak and tired, but the angels came and strengthened Him.

When He returned to Galilee the power of the Spirit of God was upon Him as He preached in the synagogues. In Capernaum sick people were healed by Jesus' power.

Then He came to His own town of Nazareth where He had been brought up. It was the Sabbath Day and everyone was in the synagogue to worship the Lord.

The book of the prophet Isaiah was given to Jesus to read. He found the place where it was written about the Saviour who was to come. Jesus read:

'The Spirit of the Lord is upon Me
Because He has anointed Me to preach the gospel to the poor.
He has sent Me to heal the broken-hearted,
To preach deliverance to the captives,
The recovery of sight to the blind,
To free the oppressed,
And to proclaim the year of the Lord's favour.'

Jesus closed the book and sat down. Everyone was looking at Him. "Today," said He, "this Scripture is fulfilled." As He preached to them they all wondered at the gracious words which proceeded out of His mouth. They said, "This *is* Joseph's son, isn't it?"

They could not believe that it was the One Who had grown up among them. They had heard that He had already healed people in Capernaum, and they hoped that He would do something wonderful in Nazareth.

Then they were angry with Him, because He performed no miracle. Jesus was taken outside the city where there was a cliff, over which they were going to throw Him. But somehow, He was lost in the crowd and walked away from the jeering mob.

The first miracle

This is the first miracle Jesus performed.

When Jesus came back from the desert places where He had been praying and where he was tempted by the devil, He passed by John the Baptist, who was with two of his disciples. "Look," said John, "this is the Lamb of God." Then the two men followed Jesus, so Jesus asked them, "What do you want?"

"We want to know where You are staying," they said.

"Come with Me, and see," Jesus replied. So they went with Jesus and stayed with Him, because they wanted to be near Him, and hear what He had to say.

One of them was Andrew. He then went and found his own brother. "We have found the Messiah," he said excitedly, and Andrew brought Simon his brother to see Jesus. When Jesus saw him He said, "You are Simon, but you will be called Peter." (Peter means a rock, or stone.)

The next day, Jesus went out and found Philip, and said to him: "Follow Me." And Philip did.

Then, Philip went and found his friend Nathanael. "Come," he said, "we have found the One of Whom Moses and the prophets have written! It's Jesus from Nazareth."

Nathanael could hardly believe that the promised Christ should come from a place like Nazareth.

"Come and see for yourself," – and Philip took his friend along to see Jesus.

When Jesus saw Nathanael, He said, "I know about you; I saw you before Philip called you, when you were sitting beneath the fig tree meditating."

Nathanael was astounded. "Teacher, You are the Son of God; You are the King of Israel!"

Jesus replied, "You are going to see and hear things more wonderful than this in the coming days."

So the Lord Jesus began to gather His disciples together. He had things He wanted to tell them. They were to be leaders in the church.

Now, the family of Jesus was invited to a wedding in Cana of Galilee, so Jesus went to the wedding with His disciples.

Wedding feasts often lasted several days, during which quite a lot of food and drink had to be provided for all who came. Everyone was happy that a new family was starting, and they wanted to wish the young man and his wife every happiness as they began a new life together in their new home. When the last day of the feast arrived, the bridegroom found that they were running out of wine. There would not be enough for everyone. What could he do? Everyone would look at him and say, "No wine? This is not a very good wedding feast. Fancy asking us all to come to a wedding and then not having enough wine for everyone!" The bridegroom felt ashamed. He was going to be very embarrassed.

Now, the mother of Jesus found out that the wine was almost gone. She believed Jesus could do something about it. When there were problems at home, He always had the right answer. She felt sure that it was time Jesus did something to prove He was Someone special, as she believed Him to be.

"They have no wine," she said to Him, hoping that Jesus would be able to help with the problem.

Then, Jesus told His mother Mary that He would do His work and the work of His Father in Heaven at the right time.

Mary went to the servants who were helping with the wedding. "If Jesus asks you to do anything," she said, "you do it."

Before long, Jesus did come to them. Standing there were six large water pots. The water in them was usually drawn out and used for the Jews to wash before they ate, as well as at other times. These pots held much water – twenty or thirty gallons. Jesus said to the servants, "Go and get water, and fill the pots up to the brim."

When they were full, Jesus said, "Now draw some out and take it to the Master of the Banquet." No one knew that the wine had all gone, except the servants. When the Master of the Banquet had tasted the wine he called the bridegroom. "This is very good wine," he told him. "Usually, they serve the best wine first, but you have saved the best until now. Very good!"

Now there was plenty of the best wine for all who wanted it, for Jesus, without touching anything, had changed all that water into wine. It had been done quietly, without any fuss or ceremony. Everyone was happy, and the disciples were shown by this first miracle of Jesus Who He was; for without the power of God no one could make so much good wine, in a moment, out of ordinary water.

Jesus visits Jerusalem

During the next three years, Jesus travelled through the country preaching in the towns and villages, speaking to the people and healing many who were ill.

At Passover, He travelled with His disciples to Jerusalem. He entered the temple courtyard and looked around. What He saw made Him angry. Instead of quiet reverence for God in His holy temple, there was shouting and a great commotion. People should have been coming with their sacrifice into the presence of the great God of all in reverence and in wonder, but inside the walls of that holy building it was like a market place. People were buying and selling. The money changers were clinking their money bags. Cages of doves were being sold to the people for their sacrifices. Sheep were bleating away in their pens. There was arguing about prices. Oxen were tied up and were adding to the din with their lowing. Jesus was not pleased.

"This is not how it should be," He said. Picking up some rope which had been used to tether the oxen, He made it into a whip and began to drive out all the animals. When He came to the money changers' tables He tipped them over. The coins ran everywhere, and to those who sold doves He said, "Take these things away. You have made My Father's House into a den of thieves." Jesus was so furious, that everyone there took their things and hurried out of the building.

No one said, "You should not do that," because they knew that He was right, but some Jews did come to Him and say, "Tell us what right You have to do all this. If you are from God show us a miracle to prove it."

Jesus answered them in a way which they did not understand. "This will be the sign for you," He said. "Destroy this temple, and in three days I will raise it up. That will be a sign to you."

"Forty-six years this temple took to build; can You raise it up in three days?" they cried in disbelief.

But Jesus meant the temple of His body. He knew that one day they would kill Him, and He also knew that after three days His body would be raised up from being dead, to being alive for evermore.

Later on, when Jesus had died on the cross, and had risen again to live forever, His disciples remembered what He had said at this time.

When the people saw Jesus and the miracles which He did in Jerusalem many of them believed in Him.

There was one man who was a ruler of the Jews. He was very interested in what Jesus did and said. He came to see Jesus one night to ask Him questions. His name was Nicodemus. "No one can do these miracles," he said to Jesus, "unless God is with him."

Jesus told Nicodemus things he had never heard before, and these he found hard to understand. Jesus explained to Nicodemus how he could come into the kingdom of God. This is one of the great statements Jesus made to this man:

"God so loved the world that He gave His only begotten Son, that whoever believes in Him should not perish, but have everlasting life."

Every Christian loves to hear these words which Jesus spoke.

On the way back to Galilee He had to go through Samaria. Now, the Samaritans did not usually have much to do with the Jews. They did not like one another.

Jesus came to a place called Sychar, and, being tired, He sat by a well while His disciples went into the city to buy some food.

A woman came along to draw water from the well. Jesus spoke to her. "Will you give Me a drink?" He asked. The woman was surprised. "You are a Jew, aren't You?" she asked. "Why do You ask me, a woman of Samaria, for a drink? Jews do not talk to us."

"If you only knew Who was talking to you," Jesus replied, "you would ask Him for something, for you are in great need."

As Jesus spoke to her about her sins she suddenly exclaimed, "Sir, I see You are a prophet!" Then Jesus talked to her about worshipping God.

She was so impressed with Jesus and what He had said, that she left her water pot at the well and ran back into the city to tell the people. As a result, they asked Him to stay with them, and many of them came to believe in Him. They said, "We know that You are the Christ, the Saviour of the world."

Jesus returns to Galilee

The people living in Galilee had heard and seen the things which Jesus had said and done in Jerusalem because many of them had been there for the Passover Feast.

When Jesus arrived back in Galilee He went to Cana, where the water had been turned into wine. Now, a certain nobleman whose son was very ill, heard that Jesus was there. This nobleman came from Capernaum, which was nearly twenty miles away, to find Jesus and ask Him to come and heal his son. The man was very worried. His son was so ill that he thought that he would probably die.

Jesus said to him, "You want only to see a sign or a wonder. You do not really believe in Me."

"Lord, come now, before my child dies," the man pleaded.

"Go back home," Jesus said, "your son is healed!"

The nobleman believed Jesus and started on his way home. The next day on his journey his servants came to meet him. "Your son is alive and well!" they said.

How happy the nobleman was! Then he asked, "At what time did he begin to get better?"

"Yesterday, at one o'clock, the fever left him," replied the servants.

Then the father knew that it was at the very time when Jesus had said to him, 'Your son is healed.'

When he arrived home he told his family and the servants what had happened. Then they all believed in Jesus.

Later, Jesus was walking by the Sea of Galilee when He saw two fishermen casting their nets into the sea. They were Peter and Andrew, his brother, who had met Jesus after He was baptized in Judaea.

"Follow Me, and I will make you fishers of men," He called.

Immediately, they left their nets and followed Jesus.

A little further along, Jesus saw two more young men. They were brothers, too, and their names were James and John. They were with their father mending their fishing nets. Jesus called them also. They did the same as the others. They left their nets and their father, and followed Jesus.

These men now went with the Lord Jesus as He journeyed throughout the province of Galilee, teaching in the synagogues, and preaching the gospel of the Kingdom, and healing people of all kinds of sickness and disease.

People heard about Jesus in other places far away, and they came to Galilee. With them came those who were ill, and those in pain, those who were paralyzed, and those who were unwell in their minds, and Jesus healed them. Crowds of people came to hear Jesus and to be healed by Him.

Now the religious leaders, the priests and the scribes, did not like all these people coming to listen to Jesus, and they said things against Him to the people.

One day, a man who was paralyzed was brought to Jesus, lying on a mattress. He could not move his legs. Jesus was in one of the houses. There was such a crowd of people that the men who were carrying him could not get into the house. They were determined that their friend should see Jesus. What could they do? Without waiting, they climbed up to the flat roof with the paralyzed man, and began to remove the tiles. As soon as there was a hole large enough they lowered the man through the roof, right in front of the Lord Jesus.

Then Jesus, seeing their faith in Him, said, "Friend, your sins are forgiven you."

The scribes and Pharisees said, "Who is this who can forgive sins? This is blasphemy. Only God can forgive sins!"

The man was still lying there. Then Jesus spoke: "Which is easier – to say, 'Your sins have been forgiven you', or to say, 'Rise up and walk'? But, to let you see that the Son of Man has power on earth to forgive sins" – Jesus then turned to the paralyzed man and said, "Rise, take your mattress and go home."

The man, who until that time could not move, instantly got up from his bed, rolled it up, and walked home, giving glory to God.

The people were struck with astonishment and awe. They said, "We have seen incredible things today."

Going outside, Jesus noticed a tax gatherer sitting at his tax office. It was his job to collect the taxes from the people for the Romans.

Jesus said to him, "Follow Me." And he did. His name was Matthew. He left his work and followed Jesus.

Matthew wanted all his friends to know about the Lord Jesus, so he made a great banquet in his home and invited them all to come, and there they all met Matthew's new Master.

A great crowd of people came to see Jesus, including Matthew's other tax gathering friends. The people did not like the men who collected taxes from them for the Roman Emperor. The Pharisees spoke to the disciples of Jesus: "Why do you eat and drink with all these awful people?"

Jesus said, "Healthy people do not need a doctor, but those who know that they are ill. I have not come to call good people to repent of their wrong ways. I have come to call sinners to repent. These are the kind of people who need Me."

In every way the priests and scribes tried to criticize the Lord Jesus, but the people always marvelled at the answers Jesus gave them. Whenever the priests thought that they had a good question which would catch Him out, the answer Jesus gave made them look silly, and they wished that they had not tried to trap Him.

At this time, Jesus went up a mountain alone to pray to His Father in Heaven about His work. He prayed all night, and when He came down He named the twelve men who were to be with Him and to learn from Him. He called them apostles.

The Lord Jesus was then surrounded by a great many people, all needing His healing touch. He looked at them all and, having many things to tell them, He made His way up the hillside, followed by His

188

disciples. When they found a suitable place Jesus began His great talk, which we call the Sermon on the Mount.

He began by saying:

"Those who know that they are poor in spirit, they are the ones who are happy and blessed, and not those who think how good and grand they are."

So He told them what kind of people would form His Kingdom. Jesus said to His listeners that it was not only what they did, but also what they thought which mattered. It is what was in their hearts which counted with God. He taught them how to pray and how they were to live if they were going to be His people.

He told them that God, who cares for the little birds and provides their food for them, cares also for all who trust in Him.

Jesus spoke to them, warning of the wide gate and the broad way which lead to destruction, that is, the easy way: as well as the small gate and the narrow way which leads to life, and how few take this difficult path.

Finally, He told the story of two men and how they built their houses. The wise man built his house on the rock and when a terrible storm came the house stood firm. But the foolish man built his house on the sand and when the storm beat upon that house, and the floods of water came up, it fell and was washed away.

"Those who listen to My words and do them," Jesus said, "are like the wise man who built his house on the rock. When the storms of life come it will stand."

The people all listened intently to His long sermon, and at the end they were amazed. "We have never heard anything like it before!" they exclaimed.

Two stories from the farm

One of the interesting things about the Lord Jesus was the way He told stories. They all had a meaning, of course, although not everyone understood what the stories meant. Many of them were told in order to show how God's kingdom would come, and how it would grow. Other stories described the way people come into the kingdom of God, or what happens to those who do not listen to the Lord's kind invitation to come.

One fine day, Jesus sat by the lakeside, but such a large crowd of people came around Him that He could not be seen. So He stepped into a boat and taught the people as they stood on the shore. This is what He said:

"A farmer went out to his field to sow his seed. As he scattered it over the field some fell on the path. The birds came and took the seed which fell there. Some seed fell on rocky ground where there was only a thin layer of earth. It sprang up quickly, but the soil was shallow and so the sun scorched the roots and it withered, because the roots could not go down deep to find moisture and nourishment. Other seeds fell among thorns and thistles and they grew up and smothered the little plants. But some of the seed fell into good ground and produced a crop, thirty times more than what was sown, or sixty times, or one hundred times more than what had been sown."

These stories were called parables. Later on, the disciples asked Jesus why He told parables. "Parables," Jesus said, "are for people like you who really want to know the secrets of the kingdom of Heaven." Jesus did not explain the meaning of all His stories; He left people to work out the meaning themselves. But He did explain the parable of the sower to His disciples to give them the idea of what His stories meant. So here is the explanation of the parable of the sower.

The parable of the sower

When people hear the message about the kingdom of God and do not pay much attention to it, the evil one comes along and snatches away what was sown in their heart. That is like the seed sown on the hard pathway. It never even began to grow.

The seeds which fell on the rocky ground did begin to grow. These seeds are like those who like what they hear, but when troubles come they wither away because their hearts are shallow and hard underneath. The word of God has not taken good root.

The seed which fell among thorns and thistles represents those who do have good roots, but the worries of life, their work and their pleasures crowd out the things of the kingdom, and there is nothing for God.

But the seed which fell on good ground shows what a person is like who hears God's Word and pays attention to it. These people bring forth a harvest for God, and some bring forth a very good harvest for Him.

The good seed

Another farming story Jesus told concerned a man who sowed good seed in his field. While everyone was asleep an enemy came and sowed weeds. When the seed began to grow, the farmer's servants found weeds which looked rather like the wheat, growing up as well.

"Shall we pull all these weeds up?" they asked.

"No," replied the farmer, "if you do that you may pull up the good wheat at the same time. Leave it until the harvest, let them both grow together until then. At that time I will tell the harvesters to separate the weeds from the wheat. The weeds will be bound together to be burned, but the wheat will be brought into my barn."

What did it mean? Jesus explained it to His disciples: the one who sowed the good seed is the Son of Man. The field is the world. The good seed represents the children of the kingdom. The weeds are the children of the wicked one. The enemy who sowed them is the devil. The harvest is the end of the world. The harvesters are the angels. At the end of the world the Son of Man will be sending His angels out to separate the weeds from the wheat. They will sort out the bad from the good, and the bad will be thrown into the fire, a place of intense pain and unhappiness. Then shall the righteous shine like the sun in the kingdom of their Father.

How sad for those who would not listen to God's voice, but how happy for those He has forgiven, and accepted into His kingdom.

Miracles

The sick servant

Not all soldiers are cruel men. There was a Roman army officer who had a servant who became very ill; it seemed that he was going to die. Now this centurion loved his men. He was also kind to the Jewish people; he had built them a synagogue in which to worship. So he asked the Jews to go to Jesus to ask Him if He would come and heal his servant. They came to Capernaum and said, "Please come, he is a good man, he loves our nation."

So Jesus went with them, but as He came near to the house some friends of the centurion met Him. They told Him, "Our master says, 'Do not trouble Yourself, I am not fit for You to come to my home, that is why I did not come myself to see You: I believe that if You just give the command my servant will be healed. You see, when I say to my servants, "Do this", or "Do that", they do it. I believe that You only need say the word, and my servant will live.'"

When Jesus heard this, He said, "This is wonderful! Here is a Roman soldier who has more faith than the people of Israel. There are going to be many people throughout the world who will come into My kingdom, while there are those from this nation who will be driven out into outer darkness for ever. How sad for them!"

To the centurion's friends He said, "Go back to the house. What you have asked has been done, for you have believed in Me."

Those who had been sent returned and found that the sick servant was now completely well.

The man at the pool

One day when Jesus was in Jerusalem He came by the pool of Bethesda. By the arches around the water there lay many sick people and those who were blind, lame and paralyzed. From time to time the water was stirred up, and they believed that whoever could get into the water first would be healed.

192

There was one man there who could not move. He had been like this for thirty-eight years. Jesus said to him, "Do you want to be made well?"

The man said, "I have no one to put me into the water when it is stirred up. Someone else always gets there before me."

"Stand up," said Jesus. "Roll up your bedding, and walk."

The man was cured. He picked up his bed and went home.

The man who died – then lived

Another day, Jesus came to a city called Nain. His disciples were with Him and a large crowd of people followed Him. As they came to the gates of the city, a dead man was being carried out to be buried. He was the only son of a woman whose husband had also died. She was weeping. When the Lord saw her He felt sad in His heart.

"Don't cry," he said. Then He went up to the wooden casket in which the dead man lay, and put His hand on it. Those carrying the casket stopped. Then Jesus said,

"Young man, I say to you – Get up!"

To the amazement of everyone, the dead man sat up. Then Jesus gave him back to his mother.

The people were filled with wonder. They praised God. "A great prophet has appeared among us," they said. "God has come to His people."

The news spread in Judaea that a dead man was now alive again.

The terrible storm

When evening came, Jesus said, "Let us go to the other side of the lake." Leaving the crowd behind, Jesus and His disciples climbed into a boat. He had been very busy and was extremely tired. It was not long before He was fast asleep. Suddenly, the wind began to blow, and the waves lifted the boat up and down. Still, the Lord Jesus slept. The wind blew and screamed and the water began to come in over the side of the boat. In the stern Jesus lay fast asleep. The disciples were frightened, the storm was so furious. "Master, Master!" they cried, "Save us, we're all going to drown!" Jesus woke up, and, seeing the raging waters, He cried, "Be still! Be quiet!"

Immediately, the wind died down, and the waves were still, and all was calm.

How surprised the disciples were! They looked at one another, they looked at Jesus. "Who is this?" they asked, "Even the strong winds and the dangerous waves obey Him!"

A worried father and a woman of faith

Then the Lord returned again to the crowds who were waiting for Him. They welcomed Him back. As soon as Jesus arrived, a ruler of the synagogue, named Jairus, came up to Jesus and, bowing down before His feet – "Please come and help me," he said, "my little girl is dying." So Jesus started to go with Jairus to see his daughter, who was about twelve years old.

So many people were crowding around, that Jesus could not get along very well. Then, a woman who had been losing blood for twelve years, touched Him. She had come up behind the Lord Jesus, saying to herself, "If only I can touch Him, I know I shall be made well."

Jesus stopped. "Who touched Me?" He asked.

"Everyone is crowding around You, people are touching You all the time," Peter said.

"Someone touched Me," Jesus said, "I know that power has gone out of Me."

When the woman realized that Jesus knew, she came forward, trembling. She then told Him, as the people were listening, that it was she herself who had touched Him, and that she felt herself healed immediately.

Then Jesus said to her, "Daughter, be of good cheer, your faith has made you well. Peace be with you."

As He said this, a message came from the house of Jairus, the ruler of the synagogue. "Your daughter is dead. You have no need to worry the Teacher now."

A sigh escaped the crowd. Jesus was too late.

But when Jesus heard this, He said, "Do not be afraid. Only believe, and she will be made well."

So they went on to the house, wondering. Friends and relations were in the house crying, but Jesus said, "Do not weep; she is not dead, but asleep." Some laughed at Him, for they knew the child was dead.

"Everyone outside!" He commanded, and taking the girl's father and mother with Him, and Peter, James and John only, He went in with them.

Holding the dead child's hand, He said, "Little girl, arise!"

She stirred as her spirit returned, then she stood up. "Give her something to eat," Jesus told them.

Her parents were astonished that their daughter, who was dead one minute was made alive and well as soon as Jesus had spoken to her.

The good news spreads

As Jesus left the home of the little girl and her happy parents to go to the house where He was staying, two blind men followed Him as best they could. "Son of David!" they cried out. "Have mercy on us!"

Jesus went into the house, but the blind men followed Him with the help of their friends.

Then Jesus said to them, "Do you believe that I am able to make you see?"

"Yes, Lord," they answered Him.

Then He touched their eyes. How wonderful for them, they could see! It was marvellous. They went out and spread the news to all around that Jesus had made them able to see again.

As Jesus went out once more among the people, a man who could not speak was brought to Him. He was cured and then he who was dumb was able to speak.

Jesus said to His disciples, "There are so many sad and unhappy people about with no one helping them. No one cares for them. There is much to be done.

"I am going to send you out on a tour of the country. As you go, preach. Say, 'The kingdom of Heaven is at hand, it is near.' I am giving you power. Heal the sick, cleanse lepers, cast demons out of people, as I do. Do not ask to be paid, and take no money with you. Do not take anything except the clothes you are wearing. When you come to a city ask for a person who will let you stay with them. When you enter the house give it your greeting, and let your peace be upon those who are kind to you. Some will not receive you: the judgment of God will be upon them.

"Not everyone will listen to you, just as they do not listen to Me. But do not fear those who ill-treat you. Your Father in Heaven even cares for the sparrows; He cares much more about you. He knows about every hair on your head. If you are telling others about Me, I will be telling My Father Who is in Heaven about you. Whoever puts Me first, before everyone else and everything else, he will not lose his

reward. Anyone who gives a little child a cup of cold water for love of Me, will not lose his reward."

Then Jesus also appointed seventy disciples to go out, two by two. When they returned to Jesus they were full of joy. They said, "Lord, even the demons obey us by Your Name!"

"Yes," said Jesus, "I saw Satan fall from Heaven. His kingdom is being defeated. But I will give you a greater reason to rejoice. Rejoice even more, because your names are written in Heaven."

After this, Jesus climbed into one of the boats and they went across the lake, or sea, of Galilee, to the other side. The people wanted to see Him and hear Him, so they walked around the lake. A great crowd came to Jesus as He climbed up a mountainside and there He talked to them, for a long time. When it was getting late, Jesus said to Philip, "These people have been out all day. They need something to eat. Where can we buy bread for them?"

"We will need a great deal of money to be able to buy even a little food for all these people."

Jesus said, "Go and see if anyone has any food with them." They came back to Jesus, and Andrew said, "There is a boy here who has five little barley loaves and two small fishes, but they will not feed this great crowd."

Jesus said, "Make everyone sit down on the grass, in groups of a hundred, and groups of fifty." In all there were about five thousand men, besides women and children.

The disciples had asked the little boy if he would give Jesus the food he had with him. So Jesus gave God thanks for what He had supplied, and began to give the bread and the fish to the disciples. He kept giving them bread and giving them fish, and giving them more bread and giving them more fish. The disciples took the food round to the people and kept coming back for more. At last, everyone had eaten enough.

"Now," Jesus said, "nothing must be wasted. Some of the people have baskets, go round and collect up all the pieces left over." They gathered up twelve baskets full of food which was left over!

The people said, "Truly, this is the Prophet who is to come into the world." And they wanted to make Him their king there and then. But Jesus made His disciples get into the boat, and whilst they were doing this He slipped away up the mountain to pray. He was not going to be that kind of a king.

Walking on the water

It was evening time, and it was becoming dark. Jesus had had a busy day. He was now up the mountain praying alone to His Father in Heaven. He had instructed His disciples to get in the boat and go back across the lake. It was a long row of about ten miles. As they were rowing, the wind began to strengthen and to blow against them. The waves became rough and boisterous. They could make little or no headway against the elements. Even though they had been struggling for hours they did not seem to be getting any nearer to the land. But Jesus saw them straining at the oars. They were tired out for they had been rowing all night. Across the waves one of them thought he could see something. Then the others saw Someone walking on the water. They were troubled, and cried out in fright. They thought it was a ghost. Then a voice called to them above the wind. "Be of good cheer, it is I. Do not be afraid!"

Then Peter spoke up: "Lord, if it is You, command me to come to You on the water!"

Jesus called, "Come."

Peter went to the side of the boat, climbed over and began to walk on the water toward the Lord. He was almost there, but when the wind gusted strongly against him, he became afraid and began to sink into the water.

"Lord, save me!" he cried. Jesus reached out His hand and lifted him back on to the waves, and they made their way to the boat. "Where is your faith? Why did you doubt?" Jesus asked Peter. As they climbed on board the wind dropped and all was calm.

All those in the boat then worshipped Jesus, saying, "Certainly, You are God's Son."

When they came to the other side and the people found that Jesus was with them, they made it known throughout the country round about, and people came with their sick folk and begged to touch just the edge of His coat, and all who touched were healed.

Who is Jesus?

Jesus had other towns and villages to visit. He and His disciples were on the way north to Caesarea Philippi. As they walked, Jesus asked His disciples a question: "Who do men say that I, the Son of Man, am?"

They answered, "Some say you are John the Baptist, whom Herod killed. You have his spirit in you. Some say that fiery spirit is in you from Elijah the prophet. Other men say that you are that sad and tender prophet Jeremiah, or one of the other prophets."

Then He said to them, "But who do *you* say I am?"

Peter was always the one to speak up. He said, "You are the Christ, the Son of the Living God."

Jesus replied, "Simon" – that was Peter's other name – "you are a blessed person to know that. This has been revealed to you by My Father in Heaven. Your name is Peter, (which means a rock), and upon this rock of your confession I will build My church. My church will be made up of those who have come to realize Who I am, and, like you, believe in Me. My church will grow and advance, and all the forces of evil will not be able to prevent it."

Now that the disciples were more sure in their minds and hearts Who Jesus was, He began to tell them other things:

"I am going to Jerusalem," He told them, "and there I am going to suffer at the hands of the elders, the chief priests and the teachers of the law. I shall be rejected, and I shall be killed. But, on the third day I will be raised to life again."

"No," exclaimed Peter, "You must not talk like that. You cannot mean that. It is unthinkable."

But Jesus knew what He had come to this world to do. He had to die if He was to save His people from their sins. That was why He came. He could not allow Peter to stop Him from that great purpose. He rebuked Peter: "Yours are the words of Satan. Do not get in My way. You do not know the mind of God. I have to die, I have to go to the cross if I am to take away the sins of the world."

Later, after saying this, Jesus called the people together.

"If you are going to follow Me," He said, "you also must deny yourself, you also must say 'No' to the things you may like, in order to follow Me. If you are going to follow Me, you will have a cross of suffering and may need to die for Me. But the day is coming when I will return with all the holy angels and receive and reward all those who have loved and served Me."

Jesus said, "The Son of Man has not come to be waited on, He has come to serve, and He has come to give His life as a ransom for many." Later on, Jesus showed them what He meant. It was the servants' work to wash the feet of their masters after they had been walking through the dusty streets in their sandals. On this occasion, Jesus Himself took a bowl of water and a towel and washed His disciples' feet. It was a lesson they did not forget. Fancy their Lord and Master washing their feet! They should have washed His!

Six days later, Jesus took Peter, James and John up a high mountain. They had no idea why the Lord should have taken them up there. It was for a very special purpose. As they were resting after their climb, the face of Jesus began to shine as brightly as the sun, and His clothes became glistening white. There appeared before them two great men who had lived many years before. They were Israel's great teacher, Moses, and Elijah, the prophet of God. The disciples stood aghast. Moses and Elijah talked with Jesus, and were speaking about His death which was to happen in Jerusalem, according to God's plan.

Then Peter said to Jesus, "Lord, this is wonderful. Let us stay here and make three shelters, one for You, one for Moses, and one for Elijah."

While Peter was speaking a very bright cloud came over them. It terrified them. Then a voice spoke out of the cloud. It said:

"This is My Beloved Son, with Whom I am well pleased. To Him you must listen."

The disciples fell down on their faces, for they were afraid. Then all was quiet.

Jesus came to them, and touched them. He said, "Arise, and do not be afraid." Looking around, they saw no one; only Jesus.

On the way back down the mountain, Jesus instructed them: "Tell no one about this until after I have died and come alive again."

It was something those three men never forgot.

When they reached the foot of the mountain, quite a different sight met their eyes. There was a boy in whom lived a demon spirit. His father came to Jesus. "Can't You help me?" he cried. "My son is very ill. Sometimes when it is bad with him, he falls into the fire, and

sometimes into the water. I brought him to Your disciples, but they cannot cure him. What shall I do?"

Just then the demon spirit threw the boy into a violent fit, and he fell to the ground. Jesus ordered the wicked spirit to come out of the boy. He was instantly healed, and Jesus gave him back to his grateful father.

When they were alone again, the disciples came to Jesus and asked Him, "Why could we not cast out the demon spirit?"

Jesus answered them, "It is because you do not have enough faith. This kind of work does not happen unless there is prayer and fasting."

The disciples were thinking more and more about Jesus as King. They were not sure what kind of kingdom it was to be. They rather thought that the Lord would raise an army and fight the Romans and drive them out of the land. They had the idea that He was going to conquer the world by His power and be the king in Jerusalem one day. Then they thought that they would be His ministers of state in the country and the world. Jesus had to teach them that His kingdom was not like that. But they did not seem to understand, however many times He told them.

One day, as they were walking together to Capernaum, they were having an argument about which of them was going to be the greatest in the kingdom. When they arrived at the house Jesus asked them, "What were you discussing on the way here?" They did not answer, but Jesus knew what it was. He called a little child to Him and lifted him up in His arms. "This little one trusts Me and his parents. Whoever trusts Me and receives Me as this little child does, he is the greatest in the kingdom of Heaven. Unless you are converted and become like little children you will not even enter My kingdom. Let no one prevent one of these little ones from coming to Me. It would be better for such a person that he had never been born."

Jesus loved boys and girls. Another day they wanted to crowd around Him, and mothers wanted Him to hold their babies. The disciples tried to send them off. "Jesus is much too busy to have all these children bothering Him," they said. But Jesus said, "No, let them come to Me. The kingdom of Heaven belongs to such as these." Then Jesus called them to Him, took them in His arms and blessed them.

How happy were these boys and girls to talk to Jesus and to know that He was their friend.

Jesus returns to Jerusalem

It was time for Jesus to leave Galilee and go to Jerusalem. On the way, as He was going through Samaria with His disciples, he met ten men outside a village who had the disease of leprosy. This disease could not usually be cured. Leprous people had to stay outside the towns and villages, away from other people, in case they too would catch the disease. So these lepers did not come near the Lord Jesus, but called to Him with a loud voice, "Jesus, Master, have mercy on us!"

Jesus called back, "Go and show yourselves to the priests." They had to do this if they thought that they were cured. If the priests could find no leprous marks on them, they let them go back again to their homes and their families.

Now, as these men were going to the priests they found that they were healed. So they ran on faster to see the priests and then go home.

But one of them stopped, turned back and gave thanks to God. He fell before Jesus and worshipped Him; and this man was a Samaritan.

Then Jesus asked, "Were not all ten of you cured? Where are the other nine?" Then He said to the Samaritan, "You are made clean in your heart, as well as your body," and Jesus sent him on his way, a new man.

Jesus told the people a story about another Samaritan. The Jews did not like the Samaritans. They did not even speak to them if they could help it. This is how Jesus came to tell the story. One of the teachers of the Jewish law asked Jesus a question which he thought Jesus would find hard to answer. The lawyer said, "Teacher, what shall I do to inherit eternal life?"

Jesus answered by asking him a question. "What does it say in the law of God? How do you read it?"

The lawyer replied, "You shall love the Lord your God with all your heart, with all your soul, with all your strength and with all your mind, and your neighbour as yourself."

"Quite right," Jesus replied. "If you do all that, you will live."

(Jesus knew that even the best people cannot always keep God's laws as they should.)

But the lawyer did not want to leave it there. He had another difficult question for Jesus.

"Who is my neighbour?" he asked.

So Jesus told this story to show him.

"There was a man going down the road from Jerusalem to Jericho, when thieves jumped out on him. They beat him up, took away his clothes and all he had, and left him on the ground half dead.

"A little later, a priest came down the road. He saw the poor man. He did not even go near him; he passed by on the other side of the road, and left him there. You would think a priest would have done something for the wounded man, wouldn't you? Then, a Levite came along." (Levites studied God's laws and assisted the priests in their work.) "The Levite did go and look at the man on the ground, but then he hurried on, too. He had other important things to do.

"Later, a Samaritan appeared." (The Samaritans usually had no dealings with the Jews, but this man could not leave that injured person there on the side of the road.) "He stopped. He spoke to him, and out of his pack he brought some soothing oil to pour into his wounds. Then, using what he had, he bandaged up the man, lifted him up on to his own horse, and took him to the nearest hotel. He looked after the poor man that night. Next morning, the Samaritan said to the hotel keeper, 'This man has been robbed and has no money. I will pay for his stay here. Please look after him. Here is some money now. If it costs any more than that, I will pay you when I come back again.'

"Now," said Jesus, "which one of those three people was a neighbour to the man who was robbed?"

The lawyer answered, "The one who showed him mercy."

"Yes," Jesus said. "Now you go and love everyone, whoever they are."

The raising of Lazarus

Not far from Jerusalem was the little village of Bethany. In that village lived two sisters, Martha and Mary. Their brother Lazarus lived with them. Martha invited Jesus to their home. They became His friends, and Jesus often stayed there. Mary loved to hear what Jesus had to say, and she often sat listening intently to His every word. But Martha was always busy tidying the house and preparing meals. One day she came to Jesus, all hot and harassed, and said to

Him, "Have you not noticed that I do all the work, while my sister does nothing? Why don't you tell her to help me?"

"Martha, Martha, you are upset and worried about many things. I do not need you to cook such grand meals. Do not fret so much. What Mary is hearing is more important than all the work of the house. People are sometimes too busy doing things for Me, when it would be better for them to listen to the words of life," said Jesus.

Some time later, Lazarus their brother became very ill, so ill that they thought he would die. The sisters sent a message to Jesus saying, "Lord, the one You love is ill."

Jesus loved Martha and her sister and Lazarus, but when He received the message He stayed where He was for two more days, before He went back to Bethany. Then He told the disciples, "Our friend Lazarus has fallen asleep. I am going to wake him up."

"If he is sleeping, then he will get better," said the disciples. But Jesus was speaking about the sleep of death, so He explained, "Lazarus is dead."

By the time Jesus arrived at the village, Lazarus had been in the tomb for four days. A great many people had come to comfort Martha and Mary. When Martha heard that Jesus was coming she got up and ran to meet Him. He was still outside Bethany. "Lord, if You had been here, my brother would not have died!" she cried. "Even now, I know that whatever You ask of God, He will do it for You."

"Your brother shall rise again from the dead," Jesus said.

"Yes," she said, "I know that he will rise again at the resurrection on the last day."

"I am the resurrection and the life," Jesus said. "Do you believe that?"

"Yes, Lord," Martha answered. "I believe You are the Christ, the Son of God."

Then she went back to the house where Mary was. She said, "The Master has come and is calling for you to see Him outside."

Mary hurried out to find Jesus. She fell down before Him and said the same as Martha had done. "Lord, if only You had been here my brother would not have died." She was crying.

So He went into the village with her, and when He saw all the people with tears in their eyes Jesus was very troubled in His heart.

"Where have you laid him?" He asked. They showed Him the cave where the body of Lazarus lay. Then Jesus also wept.

"How He must have loved him! " said some. Others said, "Could He, Who has done so many miracles, not have kept His friend from dying?"

This saddened Jesus even more, and He groaned within Himself. "Roll away the boulder from the front of the tomb," He commanded.

Then Martha said, "Lord, we cannot do that, he has been dead four days now."

Jesus looked at her. "Did I not say to you that if you believe, you will see the glory of God?"

So they moved the boulder. Then Jesus looked up and prayed. "Father in Heaven, I thank You that You have heard Me. I know that You always hear Me, but I say this so that these people here should know and believe that it is You Who have sent Me."

Jesus then called in a loud voice: "Lazarus, come out!"

From the cave in the rock where he had been laid there was a movement, and as all the people watched, Lazarus came walking out, still in the burial cloths in which he had been wrapped.

"Take off those burial cloths, and let him go," said Jesus.

Many of the Jews who had come to be with the sisters, and saw what happened, now believed in Jesus. But when the chief priests heard about this and all the other miracles which Jesus was doing they did not like it. They held a council meeting and said, "What are we going to do? Soon all the people will be following this man."

"It would be better for Him to die," the High Priests pronounced. So from that day they began to plan how they might kill Jesus.

Later, a little while before Jesus died, He did come back again to see His friends at Bethany. He was in the house of Simon who had been a leper. Lazarus was there, and Martha was the one who was preparing the supper for them all. After the meal, when they had all talked and eaten together, Mary did something very special. She had with her some very precious and very expensive perfume. Taking this, she poured it on the feet of Jesus and then wiped His feet with her hair. The whole house was filled with the scent of this very costly ointment. It was a token of her love and thankfulness to the Lord Jesus Who was soon going to die for the sins of His people.

Judas Iscariot, one of Jesus' disciples who did not really love Him, was very cross. "Why has all this expensive perfume been wasted? It could have been sold for a lot of money, which could be given to poor people." (Judas was not really concerned about the poor. He said this because he kept the apostles' money bag and he used to take some out for himself.)

"No," said Jesus. "This is a wonderful thing that Mary has done; she has poured this ointment on Me to prepare My body for burial. I tell you certainly, that wherever this gospel is preached in the whole world, people will hear about it."

The good shepherd

Jesus often made people understand what He was like by comparing himself to other kinds of people or things they knew. Everyone knew about shepherds in Palestine, so one day He said, "I am like a shepherd and those who follow Me are My sheep. I look after them and they know Me. They will not come when strange people or thieves call them, for they do not know their voice, but they know the voice of their own shepherd. The person who is paid for looking after the sheep does not love them, but I love My sheep so much that I am ready to die for them to save them. I am the good shepherd, and I know all My sheep and they follow Me. No one will ever take them away from Me, and they will never perish."

Then He said, "I am the door of the sheepfold." What He meant was this: when the night came the shepherd would gather all his sheep into the fold where they would be safely fenced in to prevent wild animals from attacking them, and where they would be kept from sheep thieves who might steal them. At the entrance to this enclosure was a gap where the shepherd would lie down. He was the door to keep his sheep safe and to protect them from all danger. "I will look after all My sheep – those who come in through the door. I am the door. If anyone enters in by the door he shall be saved."

Another time Jesus said, "Suppose one of you has one hundred sheep and you find that one of them has strayed away from the flock and become lost, what would you do? Would you not go and search for that lost one? Would you not climb the mountains and search in the valleys, among the rocks and the thickets? And if you found it fallen down on to some ledge of rock, would you not risk your life to rescue it? And when you had found it bleating away, tired and hurt, would you not lay it on your shoulders and carry it home, so happy that you had found your poor lost sheep? Then you would call your friends and say, 'Rejoice with me, I have found my sheep that was lost!'

"That," said Jesus, "is what it is like when I find a sinner who repents of his sins. There is great joy in Heaven over everyone who, having gone astray, is then found and saved."

A happy father

Here is another of the stories Jesus told.

There was a man who had worked hard, employed servants, and owned a nice house. He also had two sons who worked with him on the farm.

One of his sons grew tired of working every day; he wanted to go out and see the world, and have a good time. He said to his father, "One day, father, when you are gone, my brother and I will have all that is yours. I do not want to wait until that time. Please may I have my share now? You have done very well. Why can I not have my portion while I am still young? I want to go to other places and not stay around here for ever."

The father was sad that his son did not want to be with him in the homestead. He was unhappy because his son did not want to work with him in the family business. The father knew that it was not the best for his son to go away with his money, but, sadly, he let him go. He shared his money out between his two sons, and the one who wanted to travel took his inheritance and went on a journey to a far country.

There in the big city he soon spent his money on all kinds of pleasures. "What a good time I am having," he thought, until one day he found that he had used up all his money. The trouble was that at this time there came a famine in the land, and food, if one could get it, was very expensive. What could he do? He would starve to death and die in a foreign country. How miserable he was. At last, he found a job. He had to feed a farmer's pigs on whatever scraps could be found. He was so hungry that he could have eaten the pods and peelings himself. Day by day he grew thinner and thinner, and more miserable. No one loved him, and no one gave him anything. How stupid he had been to leave his lovely home and kind father. As he thought about it he said to himself, "My father's servants back home have plenty to eat, and I am dying of hunger. I wonder, should I go back home? Will my father be angry with me for wasting his money? I have been a fool. If I go back and tell my father what I have done, if

I say to him, 'I have sinned against Heaven and against you, I am not worthy, I do not deserve to be called your son, let me be like one of your servants' – will he have me back as one of his servants?"

So the young man decided that is what he would do. The fine clothes he had bought were now dirty and ragged as he made the long journey homeward. At last, he came in sight of his father's house. It seemed a long while since he had so jauntily strode away from his old home.

But every day, his father had prayed for his boy, and every day he had looked down the road to see if he was coming back. His heart was heavy and sad. But as he looked down the road that day he saw a figure in the distance. He thought it was his son. He looked again. He was sure it was his beloved son returning. He left the house and ran to meet him. As they met he gave his son a great hug and kissed him, he was so pleased to see him back again.

The boy began to say what he had planned to say to his father: "Father, I have sinned against Heaven and against you and do not deserve to be called your son any more . . ." But the father did not let him finish. "Quickly," he said to his servants, "let him have a good bath and then get out the best robe and put it on him, and put a ring on his finger, and bring sandals for his feet – look, his shoes are worn out! Get that calf we have been fattening, and kill it, and let's make a feast and be merry together! See, this son of mine was dead and is alive again, he was lost, and is now found." And so the party began.

Now there was one person who was not very happy. It was the other son. He was working out in the field when his brother arrived home. As he came near the house he heard music and dancing. No one had told him that there was going to be a party. He called one of the servants. "What is all this about? What's happening?" he asked.

"Your young brother has come home safe and sound, and your father is so pleased, he has killed the fatted calf and we are making merry."

The older brother scowled and was angry. He would not go in to see his brother or enjoy the party. He stayed outside and sulked.

His father came out to see him. "Do come in," he said. "Your brother has come home!"

"Father!" the older son answered crossly. "I have served you faithfully all these years. I have never left home and wasted all your money, but you have never made me a great feast like this!"

"My son," said his father, "we have always been together and all that I have has been yours. Now your brother has been in trouble, he was dead to us, but is now alive and with us; he was lost, but now he is found. We must be glad and rejoice together."

How glad is the heart of our Father God when people come to Him for forgiveness after they discover how silly and stupid and sinful they have been.

The little man

As Jesus was going toward Jerusalem where He had told His disciples He would be killed by His enemies, He came to the city of Jericho. A great crowd of people thronged around Him. One man particularly wanted to see Jesus, but being a very small man, he could not get near. So he ran on ahead and climbed up into a sycamore tree. His name was Zacchaeus, and he was one of those people the Jews did not like, for he was a tax-collector. He was a chief tax-collector, and he was very rich. Zacchaeus did get a good view of Jesus as He came along. But he would really have liked to speak to Him. Just as the Lord came by where Zacchaeus was on the branch of the tree, Jesus stopped and looked up at him. "Zacchaeus," He called, "come down quickly, I want to stay at your house today."

How happy Zacchaeus was! He had so much wanted to see and talk with Jesus, and now He was coming to his own house. Then Zacchaeus had something to tell Jesus. He knew that there were things which were not right in his life. He said, "Lord, I will give half my possessions to feed the poor who do not have enough to eat, and if I have taken anything from anyone when I should not have done, I will give them back four times as much."

What a difference it makes when people meet the Lord Jesus. Jesus said, "The Son of Man has come to seek and to save that which was lost. Today salvation has come to your house, Zacchaeus, for, like Abraham, you are a person of faith."

The wedding feast

The chief priests did not like it. Jesus had been suggesting that many of the bad people, the people whom everyone knew were really bad, would be coming into the kingdom of God, because they had listened to God's invitation to come to Him for forgiveness of their sins. But what upset the priests even more, was that Jesus had said that they would find themselves outside God's kingdom, for even their hearts were not right in God's sight. "Fancy suggesting that these bad people will be accepted, and not us!" So Jesus told them another story about the kingdom of Heaven.

"A rich man had told many of his friends that he would soon give a great banquet," Jesus began. "When all the wonderful food was nearly ready, he sent his servants to invite them to come and feast with him. But one after another, they refused to come. 'Excuse me,' one said, 'but I must go and inspect some property I have just bought.' Another had an important meeting elsewhere planned. A third had just got married.

"These were all good excuses, but still, the rich man got angry when his servants returned to the banquet hall with its rich smells of delicious hot dishes – with nobody!

"Then the rich man realized that other people who were rich were liable to be too busy to celebrate and enjoy life. But the poor, now! They would stop anything else they were doing for some free food – let alone for a banquet. 'Forget about all those people who have so much – they'll never come to taste one bite of what I prepared for them. Go and invite the poor, the homeless, the hungry, the outcasts. Let my banquet hall be filled!'

"And so it was," Jesus concluded.

When Jesus had finished the story the priests said, "He is talking about us," and they hated Him the more and tried to catch Him out with clever questions. If they could make Him say the wrong thing they could take Him away and accuse Him before the judges, and turn the people away who were listening to Him. But every question was answered with such wisdom that it made the people marvel at the wonderful words which Jesus spoke.

Then Jesus had some very severe words to say to the scribes and the Pharisees because they would not receive Him or His words. He knew that the day was soon coming when they would kill Him.

He told His disciples that before very long He would be leaving them.

"Do not be troubled, you believe in God, believe also in Me. In My Father's house are many dwelling places. I am going to prepare a place for you there. I will be coming back again to receive you to Myself and we will all be together," He told them.

Jesus said that He would be coming back as the King in all His glory and with His holy angels. "You must always be ready, for no one knows when I will be coming."

Then He told them another story of a wedding:

There were ten bridesmaids all dressed up and ready to meet the bridegroom who had a long way to come. When it was announced that he had arrived at the village they were to take their lamps and go out to meet him. But it was a long time before he came, and they all grew drowsy and fell asleep. At midnight there was a cry – "He is coming!" All the bridesmaids arose, and trimmed their lamps. Five of them had no oil in their lamps and had to go and find some. By the time their lamps were ready, it was too late. "You must be ready for Me to come at any time," said Jesus. "It is no good trying to get ready when I come. Only those who were ready went into the wedding feast."

The King comes

The time had come for Jesus to be welcomed into the city of Jerusalem by all those who loved Him. He did not come on a fine war horse, nor in a chariot as an earthly king would have done. No, He came on a humble donkey, as the Old Testament prophet had said He would.

As Jesus neared the Mount of Olives, he spoke to His disciples:

"As you enter the village you will see a donkey tied up to a door. Bring it to Me."

The disciples found the animal exactly as Jesus had said, and brought it to Him. Some of them put their coats on the donkey, and Jesus sat on these as He began His journey down the hill. Once He stopped and looked at the city before Him. Tears were in His eyes as He said, "If only you knew Who it was that was coming, you would have great peace. But you do not know, you will kill the One who is being sent to you. This city will be destroyed; not one stone will be left on top of another because you did not know your Lord had come to you."

Then He came up into the city. A great crowd was with Him. They cut down palm branches and spread them in the roadway for Him.

Some of the Pharisees did not like what was happening at all. They went up to Jesus and said to Him, "Do You hear what these people are saying about You? Tell them to stop saying such things."

Jesus answered them, "If the people were silent these stones would have to cry out their praises to God for what you are seeing today."

Others in the city asked, "Whoever is this?" The people said, "Jesus, the prophet from Nazareth."

This was the last week before Jesus' death. Each day He came to the temple and taught the people, and each evening He went out of the city to stay with His friends at Bethany, or spend the night on the Mount of Olives nearby.

The chief priests would have liked to arrest Jesus, but so many people were crowding around Him and listening to Him that they dared not touch Him. Besides, they could find no good reason to stop Him.

As Jesus was coming into Jerusalem on one of those mornings He saw a fig tree, and being hungry, He went up to it to find a fig to eat. As He searched among its branches He could not find one, only leaves. "This tree," said Jesus, "shall never again bear figs."

When He entered the temple, Jesus found that they were buying and selling and changing money, as they had done when He was there before. There was noise and hubbub, and arguing and shouting. Once more, Jesus stopped it all and turned the money tables over. "Take all these things out!" He cried. "God says in the scripture, 'My house shall be called a house of prayer for all nations', but you have turned it into a robbers' den."

This made the scribes and Pharisees determined to destroy the Lord Jesus, but they were afraid to do anything because the people loved to hear Him and what He taught.

As they went back to Bethany that evening the disciples noticed that the fig tree on which there had been no fruit, had died. During the day it had withered. It reminded them of the parable Jesus had told them about a man who had a fruit tree. For three years he had been hoping to find fruit growing, but none had appeared. "Cut it down," he told his servants. "Of what use is it?" Jesus had been preaching to, and healing people for three years now. The leaders of Israel had not listened to Him, the time was coming for the blessing of God upon their nation to be taken away from them.

One day, Jesus sat down by the chest into which the people dropped their offering money as they came to worship in the temple. Many of the rich people were putting in quite a lot. Then a very poor lady came along. She dropped in two coins.

Jesus called His disciples to Him, and said to them, "You see that poor widow? She put only two little coins into the offering box. But really she has put in more than everyone else. All the others have plenty of money left for themselves, but she has nothing. She has given it all to the Lord."

During that last week Jesus taught the people and told His disciples many things about the Kingdom of God. One day He took them to the Mount of Olives and told them what was going to happen.

"In two days' time," He said, "it will be the Passover, and I shall be taken by the chief priests and crucified. But the gospel of the kingdom will be preached in all the world before the end of all things comes. Then, I shall come back in power and great glory with all the holy angels, and I will gather My people to Me forever. I have told you before it happens. Be ready, and hold fast your faith in Me, until I come."

The last supper

The chief priests and elders were having a meeting in the palace of the High Priest. They were plotting together to arrest Jesus at a time when the crowds were not with Him. Then they had a surprise. One of Jesus' own disciples, one of the twelve, came to see them. It was Judas Iscariot. He came to betray his Lord, and help them to take Him. He agreed to tell them when they could capture Jesus, and where they could find Him when crowds of people were not surrounding Him.

"What will you give me," he asked, "if I do this?"

They agreed to give him thirty pieces of silver. So they paid Judas and he then began to look out for a good opportunity to betray the Lord. Why should Judas want to do such a thing? He did not really love the Lord Jesus, he was interested only in the money.

Now it was time for everyone to get ready for the Passover Feast. The disciples came to Jesus and asked Him, 'Where shall we prepare for You to eat the Passover?" Jesus sent Peter and John into the city and told them, "A man will meet you carrying a pitcher of water. Follow him into the house where he is going, and say to the owner of the house, the Teacher says, 'Where is the room where I am to eat the Passover with My disciples?' He will show you a large upstairs room which will be all ready for us. Prepare the Passover there."

They found everything as Jesus had said, and when the time came they all gathered around the table. Jesus said, "I have had a great desire to eat this Passover with you before I suffer."

Then Jesus took some bread, gave thanks to God, and broke it. He then said these strange and wonderful words:

"This is My body, which is going to be broken for you. Take it, and eat it. I want you to do this in remembrance of Me."

Then, He took the cup and gave thanks to God.

"This is My blood which is going to be shed for many for the forgiveness of their sins. Drink from this cup, all of you. As often as you do this together it will remind you of My death."

While they were eating Jesus said something they could hardly believe. "I am going to be betrayed," He said, "and it is one of you here who is going to betray Me." They were horrified. "Could it be me?" they all asked. No one could think that any of them could do such a thing. But Jesus said to Judas, "What you are going to do, do quickly."

Then, Satan entered into the heart of Judas and he left the table and went out. Judas knew that Jesus would be going to the Mount of Olives. He was now going to tell the priests. The other disciples had no idea where Judas had gone, or what was going to happen.

After this, they sang a hymn together and went out of the city toward the Mount of Olives.

On the way, Jesus said, "You are all going to run away and leave Me tonight. 'When the shepherd is struck down the sheep are all scattered.' That is what the prophet Zechariah said would happen."

"Oh no!" said Peter. "Even though everyone else leaves You, I will never desert You."

Jesus looked at Peter. "I will tell you the truth, Peter," He said. "This very night, before the cock crows, you will deny that you ever knew Me. In fact, you will deny Me three times. Satan wants to see if you really love Me, but I have prayed for you, for I know the test is coming."

Peter replied, "Lord, I will never leave You, even if I must die with You, I will not deny You. I will always be loyal to You."

All the disciples said the same.

Then Jesus stopped by the way and gathering the disciples around Him, He spoke some of His last words to them before He was taken away from them:

"I am going to My Father," He said, "and you will be sad, but I am going to send a Helper to you. You will not see Him, but He will be with you. It is to be the Holy Spirit of God. He will give you power to serve Me. He is the Spirit of truth. When He comes you will understand many things you do not now know. He will come to comfort you and make you strong for the work you have to do. He will be with you instead of Me, and He will be in you. My Father loves you because you have loved Me and know that I came from My Father, and now I am going back to Him. I am now going to leave you, but I will see you before I go back to My Father."

Then Jesus prayed to His Father in Heaven: "Father, the hour has come. I have done the work You gave Me to do. These are the ones You have given Me. I have given them Your word and they believe that You sent Me. I am leaving them in the world. Holy Father, keep them by Your power. I am praying also for all those who will come to

believe in Me through their message. As You sent Me into the world I am now sending them into the world. May they love one another, knowing that You love them with that great love that You have always had for Me. May Your love be in them, and may they be one together, as We are one together. I want them all to be with Me and to see My glory which I had with You before the world began.''

Betrayed!

When Jesus had finished praying, He led His disciples over the brook Kidron to the foot of the Mount of Olives, where there was an olive grove. It was called the Garden of Gethsemane.

He said to His disciples, "Stay here while I go to pray." He took Peter, James and John along with Him.

Then Jesus was terribly distressed. He said to them, "I am deeply troubled in My soul. My heart is so sad, it is broken with grief. Be with Me while I pray." Then Jesus went forward a little way, threw Himself on the ground and prayed: "My Father, if it is possible, do not let this horrible thing happen to Me." Jesus prayed long and hard. It was late and the disciples were tired. They fell asleep.

Jesus came back to them and said, "Could you not watch and pray with Me for one hour at this time? Keep watching and praying with Me. The time of testing is coming. Your spirits are willing, but your bodies are weak."

Then Jesus went back to pray again in the same way: "Father, if this is what I have to do, I will do it. Your will be done."

Going to His disciples, He found that He had been praying alone, they had fallen asleep again. Jesus went back a third time. So earnest and terrible was His praying that great drops of sweat were falling from Him, like blood. Then an angel appeared, strengthening Him in His hour of need.

Jesus went to His disciples who were again asleep. "Are you still sleeping?" He asked. "Let us get up and go. The one who has betrayed Me into the hands of sinners is here."

A crowd of soldiers and others with swords and sticks appeared, carrying lanterns, and led by Judas. He had told them that the one whom he would kiss was the one to be seized and taken away.

Judas said, "Rabbi!" and went up to Jesus and kissed Him. Jesus said, "Judas, are you betraying the Son of Man with a kiss?"

Then the disciples attempted to defend their Master, and Peter struck the servant of the High Priest with his sword and cut off his right ear.

"No more of this!" Jesus commanded His disciples. "Put your swords away. If I want protection I can ask My Father and He will send Me armies of angels to look after Me." Then He restored the man's ear to its place again.

His disciples all ran off to escape for their lives, but Jesus allowed the officers to bind Him and take Him away as a prisoner.

They brought Him in the night to the palace of the High Priest. There the scribes and elders were gathered together to try Him.

Inside, the priests were faced with a problem. They did not know with what crime they should charge Jesus, for He had done nothing wrong. They asked Him questions about His teaching.

Jesus answered, "Why are you questioning Me? I have taught nothing in secret. Everyone knows what I preached in the synagogues. What have I done wrong? What wrong things have I spoken?"

One of the officers struck Jesus a blow because He was not answering the High Priest as he wanted.

Then they called different people to say what Jesus had taught unlawfully, but none of the witnesses agreed together. They all said different things. The priests could not find any reason to put Jesus to death.

At last, the High Priest asked Jesus on oath: "Tell us, are You the Christ, the Son of God?"

Jesus said, "You are saying so, and I will tell you that you are going to see the Son of Man sitting at the right hand of God, and coming in the clouds of Heaven."

The High Priest was enraged. He tore his robe, and said: "Did you hear that? He has blasphemed! He deserves to die!"

Then they spat in His face and slapped Him, and beat Him with their fists.

It was still night time. Peter was outside when one of the servant girls noticed him. "You were with Jesus of Galilee," she said.

"I do not know what you are talking about," Peter replied.

Then, another servant girl said, "This man was with Jesus of Nazareth."

"No I was not," said Peter again, "I do not know the Man."

A third person came up to Peter. "Surely, you are one of them. I know by the way you speak."

Peter began then to curse and swear. "I do not know this Man. I am not one of His disciples."

Just then, the Lord turned and looked at Peter, and the cock began to crow. Then Peter remembered what Jesus had said to him. He got up and went away, crying bitterly. He had denied His Lord.

Crucified

As the Romans ruled the land, the Jews could not put Jesus to death unless Pilate the Governor found the prisoner guilty. In the morning therefore the Jews took Him to Pilate's court.

Pilate asked, "Of what crime is this man accused?" They answered, "He has been leading our people astray. He has said that they should not pay taxes to Caesar the Emperor; and He claims to be Christ, a king."

Jesus did not answer His accusers, and Pilate asked Him, "Are You not going to say anything to defend Yourself?" Then he asked Jesus, "Are You the king of the Jews?"

Jesus answered, "My kingdom is not of this world. If My kingdom were of this world, My servants would fight and deliver Me from the Jews."

When Pilate learned that Jesus was from Galilee, he sent Him to Herod who ruled that area. Herod was in Jerusalem just then. He hoped to see Jesus perform some miracle, but Jesus did nothing, and said nothing. Herod's soldiers ill-treated Jesus and mocked Him by putting on Him the purple robe of a king. After this, He was sent back to Pilate.

In the meantime, when Judas saw that Jesus was condemned, he was filled with horror and remorse for what he had done. He went back with his money to the chief priests and elders and said to them, "I have sinned. Jesus is innocent. I have been with Him for three years. He has never done anything wrong, only good. He should not die. Do not kill Him."

"We have Him now," they said, "whether guilty or innocent, He is in our power. You have your money – be gone!"

As Judas stood there he realized the terrible thing which was happening. He did not want the money now. He hated it; he hated what he had done. Jesus was not going to save Himself, and no one cared. With an awful look on his face, he threw the money down on the floor, and went out. He killed himself by hanging.

Jesus was again brought before Pilate. Again the Governor

questioned Him, and then called the Jews. "I can find no fault with Jesus, nor can Herod. It is my practice to release a prisoner at the Feast. There is that criminal Barabbas who tried to cause a rebellion in the land, or there is Jesus. Shall I have Jesus whipped, and then release Him?"

"No, give us Barabbas! Crucify Jesus!" they shouted. "Crucify Him! Crucify Him!"

Pilate brought out a bowl of water, and washed his hands in front of the crowd, to show them that he would have nothing to do with the condemning of an innocent man. Then he had his soldiers lash Jesus with a whip. He allowed them to make a crown from long thorns which they cruelly pressed down on His head. They covered His face and struck Him, saying, "Tell us, which one hit You!" Then they took off the robe which they had put on Him, and led Him out to be crucified.

Jesus was worn out, weak, and almost exhausted. He stumbled and fell as He carried His heavy cross to the place called Calvary. They made a man called Simon of Cyrene carry it for Him up the hill. A crowd of people followed, some jeering. Many women were crying as Jesus was led away. When they arrived at the place they nailed Jesus by His hands and feet to the cross of wood. A notice written in three languages was put on the cross, which read:

THIS IS THE KING OF THE JEWS.

When the chief priests saw that, they asked Pilate to alter it. He said, "What I have written, I have written."

Jesus had to hang there a long time before He died. "Forgive them, Father," He prayed, "for they do not realize what they are doing."

Some mocked Him. The rulers said, "He saved others, let Him save Himself, if He is the Christ of God!"

Two criminals, one on each side of Him, also mocked Him. "If You are the Christ, save Yourself and us," one said in his misery.

But the other had a change of heart, and called to his friend: "We deserve to suffer for what we have done, but this Man has done nothing wrong." Then he said to Jesus: "Jesus, remember me when You come into Your kingdom." How glad Jesus was to hear this man whose faith was in Him at this time. "I am telling you truly," Jesus answered, "Today, you will be with Me, in paradise."

Sitting there, the soldiers were gambling to see who was to have Jesus' clothes. There were many women who loved Him and followed Him, looking on at a distance. The Lord's mother was there, and

Mary Magdalene, with Mary the mother of James and Joseph, and the mother of Zebedee's sons. When Jesus saw his mother there, and John the disciple whom He loved, He said, "There is your son," and, to John, "There is your mother." So John took care of Jesus' mother and looked after her in his own home, from that day onwards.

Then a great darkness came over all the land for three hours, as if God's creation was mourning for Him.

Four more things Jesus was to say: "I am thirsty." Then, in a loud voice He called out: "My God, My God, why have You forsaken Me?"

After that: "Into Your hands I commend My spirit," and finally, with a great cry – "It is finished!"

An earthquake shook the land. The centurion who was guarding Jesus, and those who were with him, were afraid. The centurion said, "Truly, this was the Son of God."

He is risen!

Joseph of Arimathea was a good man, and had become a disciple of the Lord Jesus. He was a rich man and a council member who had not agreed with what they had done to Jesus the Christ.

Not far from where Jesus was crucified Joseph had his own new tomb in a garden. It was cut out from the rock. Joseph went with his friend Nicodemus to see Pilate to ask for permission to bury the body of Jesus there. So they took the body down from the cross and wrapped it in a clean linen cloth, and laid it in the tomb. Nicodemus brought with him a mixture of sweet smelling spices – expensive myrrh and aloes – with which to embalm the body of Jesus. Mary Magdalene and Mary the mother of James and Joses, with some of the other women who had followed Jesus from Galilee, watched and saw where the body was laid. A great stone was rolled over the entrance, and they all went home.

The Jews knew that Jesus had said that He would rise from the dead, and so they went to Pilate and asked him if he would put a seal on the stone to ensure that none of His disciples came to take His body away and then say that He was alive. "May we also have a guard of soldiers, Sir?" they asked.

Pilate agreed, and gave them soldiers to guard the tomb.

The next three days were the holy worship days of the feast. Jesus, the prophet of God, Who had done so much good and spoken so many wonderful words, was dead. His many friends were sad and bewildered. What had happened? And why had it happened?

On the first day of the week some of the women wanted to go to the tomb to see the place where their beloved Lord was laid. Mary Magdalene and Joanna, and Mary the mother of James, agreed to go early to the tomb and finish embalming the body of Jesus with oils and spices. It was dark when they started out and as they went they asked, "Who shall roll away the stone for us?" The sun was rising when they arrived. There were no soldiers on guard and the heavy stone was rolled away from the entrance to the tomb. What had happened?

Before the women had arrived, while it was still dark, there had been an earthquake and an angel of the Lord had descended from Heaven and come and rolled away the stone. The guards were terrified and shook with fear. They had hurried away, and coming into the city, they reported what had happened at the tomb. The chief priests and the elders held a meeting and decided that the best thing they could do would be to instruct the guards to say to the people that the disciples came in the night and stole the body of Jesus. Having told the guards what to say, they gave them a large sum of money. So that is the story that these guard soldiers told, although they knew that it was not true.

Then the women saw the angel, who spoke to them: "Do not be afraid. I know that you are looking for Jesus Who has been crucified. He is not here; He has risen, just as He said He would. Come and see the place where He was lying. Then go and tell His disciples and Peter: 'You will see Him in Galilee'."

The women were astonished, and trembling with excitement and fright, they ran back to the disciples to tell them the news. "The body of the Lord has gone," they said. The disciples could not believe it. Then Peter and John left the others and ran to the tomb to see for themselves. Looking in, they saw the linen in which Jesus had been wrapped, lying there by itself. They returned to the others, amazed.

Mary Magdalene came back to the tomb and stood outside crying. She became conscious of a Person in the garden whom she supposed was the gardener. She said to him, "Sir, if you have moved Him tell me where you have laid Him, and I will take Him away." She did not realize that it was Jesus Himself. Then He said to her, "Mary!" She turned and looked at Him. "Rabboni!" she exclaimed.

Jesus said, "Do not cling to Me, for I have not yet ascended to My Father; but go and tell My brothers, and say to them that I am going to ascend to My Father and your Father."

Then Mary went and told the disciples that she had seen the Lord.

That same day two of Jesus' disciples were walking to a village called Emmaus, about seven miles from Jerusalem. They were talking together about everything that had happened. As they discussed these things with each other, Jesus came alongside them and walked with them. But they did not recognize Him.

"What are you discussing so earnestly together which makes you so sad?" He asked.

Then one of them, named Cleopas, said: "You must be the only person in Jerusalem who does not know what has happened there these past days."

"What things do you mean?" asked Jesus. They said, "About Jesus of Nazareth. He was a great prophet Who did and said mighty things. Our chief priests and rulers handed Him over to be condemned to death. He was crucified. We had hoped that He was the One who would redeem Israel. That was three days ago, and now some women who went to His tomb early this morning amazed us. They could not find His body. They related to us that they had seen an angel who told them that Jesus was alive again. Others went to the tomb and found that it was just as the women had said."

Jesus said to them: "O foolish ones, how slow you are to believe! Do you not remember what the prophets have written? They tell us that the Christ should suffer and afterwards enter into His glory." Then, beginning with Moses and all the prophets, He explained to them all the scriptures about Himself. They had never heard anything like it before. What He said was so wonderful.

As they came to the village where they were going, Jesus made as if He was going on farther. "Come in and stay with us," they said. "It is getting late in the day now. We would like you to stay the night with us."

So He went in. He sat down at the table with them, and took the bread, gave thanks to God, broke it, and was giving it to them when they suddenly realized Who He was. Then He disappeared out of their sight.

They looked at each other in stunned surprise. "Did not our hearts burn within us as He talked with us along the way and explained the scriptures to us?" they asked. "We must tell the others."

They were so excited that they straightaway returned all the way to Jerusalem. When they arrived the eleven disciples were just as excited. "The Lord Himself has appeared to Peter," they said. Then the two told the others how Jesus had walked and talked with them also, and how they recognized Him when He broke bread with them.

While they were still talking Jesus Himself appeared, standing with them. "Peace be with you," He said.

His unexpected appearance startled them and made them afraid. They thought it was a ghost. Jesus spoke to them.

"Why are you frightened? Why are you doubting whether it is Me, or not? See My hands and My feet. A ghost does not have flesh and bones like this. Touch Me and see." Then He showed them His hands and His feet, where the nails had been driven through. They were filled with amazement and then with joy, hardly knowing whether to believe it or not.

Jesus then talked to the disciples about the scriptures and explained to them how all the things written in the Old Testament were all being fulfilled by what had happened to Him. So they began to understand the old writings which showed that Christ was to suffer and afterwards rise up from the dead on the third day, so that repentance and forgiveness of sins could be preached to all peoples. "You are to make these things known, but wait until I send you power from on high according to the promise of My Father."

Now Thomas was not with them when Jesus appeared. "We have seen the Lord!" they exclaimed excitedly, when he joined them later.

"I don't believe it," he replied. "Unless I see the nail marks in His hands and actually put my finger where they were, and unless I put my hand into His side where the soldier thrust in his spear, I will not believe it."

A week later the disciples were all together again in the house, and Thomas was with them this time. The doors were locked, but Jesus came and stood among them, and said:

"Peace be with you."

Then He said, "Thomas, come and look at My hands and put your finger here, and put your hand into My side. Stop doubting, and believe."

Thomas was taken aback. Jesus knew the very words he had spoken!

"My Lord, and my God!" was all he could say.

Jesus said, "You now believe, because you have seen Me. Blessed are all those who will never see Me as you have seen Me, yet they will believe."

During the next few weeks Jesus was often seen by His many disciples. Once, over five hundred saw Him at one time!

Jesus had told His disciples that they would see Him in Galilee. So after all the things that had happened in Jerusalem, they went back to their homes in Galilee.

Peter said to the others, "I'm going fishing." They said, "We will come with you." So they boarded the boat. All night they heaved out the nets and hauled them in again. When morning came they had caught nothing.

As it became light they could see Someone was standing on the shore. "Have you caught any fish, friends?" He called.

"Not a thing," they answered.

"Throw your net on the other side of the boat. You will find some there." They thought that they would try it, and, to their surprise, they immediately caught a great number of fish.

John said to Peter, "It is the Lord!" Peter immediately jumped into the water to go to Jesus. They dragged the net of fish ashore and found that Jesus had lit a fire and there was fish cooking and bread all ready for them.

They found that their catch was of all large fish, one hundred and fifty-three of them!

After they had eaten their breakfast Jesus said to Peter, "Peter, do you love Me?"

"Yes, Lord, You know that I love You."

Jesus asked him the question three times, and then said: "Feed, look after My sheep. Care for those who follow Me."

For forty days Jesus showed His disciples that He was alive. Then the time came for Him to go back to His Father in Heaven. This is what happened.

He appeared to them for the last time in Jerusalem and then led them out to the Mount of Olives where He had talked with them many times before. There He spoke to them His last words: "Do not leave Jerusalem, but stay here now and wait for the Holy Spirit to come over you as My Father has promised. That which has been promised will happen. John baptized you in water, but now in a few days' time you will be baptized in the Holy Spirit."

"Lord," they asked excitedly, "Is this the time when You are going to restore Israel's kingdom?"

Jesus replied, "That is not for you to know. The Father in Heaven has all these times in His own control; He will look after that. What you are to do, when the Holy Spirit has come upon you, is to go and tell everyone about Me here in Jerusalem, then in all Judaea and Samaria, and right throughout the whole world.

"Wait in Jerusalem for the Holy Spirit of power to come upon you," He told them. Then, lifting up His hands, He blessed them. While He was doing that He was taken away into Heaven, and he disappeared into a cloud. As they stood gazing into the sky, two men in white clothing stood beside them. "Men of Galilee," they said, "Why are you still looking into the sky? This same Jesus you have watched go into Heaven will come back again as you have seen Him go."

Then they worshipped Him and returned to Jerusalem filled with joy, and were continually in the temple praising God.

The Holy Spirit comes

The disciples were on their own now. Jesus had gone, but He had promised to be with them always. He had also promised that the Holy Spirit would come to them to strengthen them.

In Jerusalem they gathered in an upstairs room to pray. The eleven apostles, together with some of the women and Mary the mother of Jesus, were there.

First of all, they needed to choose someone in place of Judas. Peter told them, "It says in the psalms concerning the wicked, 'Let his office be taken by another.' For the office of an apostle, it is necessary for the person to have been with Jesus from the time He was baptized by John, until the day He was taken up from us. The person has to have seen Jesus after He was raised from the dead."

So they chose two, and could not decide which was the right one. They prayed, and said: "O Lord, show us which one of these men is the one You have chosen." Then, as their custom was, they drew lots, and the one chosen was Matthias.

The people of Israel came every year to worship at the temple in Jerusalem at the feast of the Passover. That is when Jesus died. Seven weeks later, the people came again to Jerusalem to worship at the feast of Pentecost. That is when the Holy Spirit came.

The disciples were together in Jerusalem at the time of the feast of Pentecost. Suddenly, the sound of a strong wind blowing violently came from Heaven, and filled the house where they were sitting. Tongues of fire appeared and settled on each of them, and they were all filled with the Holy Spirit. Then they started to speak in other languages.

Now there were in Jerusalem at that time many Jews who had come from other lands. They had come to worship in the temple, at the feast. These people were astounded to hear the men from Galilee speaking in their own languages, declaring the wonderful things God had done. They were really perplexed. Some said, "These men have had too much to drink!"

Then Peter stood up with the other disciples and began to preach.

"Let me explain to you, listen to me," he said. "We are not drunk, as you seem to think. It is only nine o'clock in the morning. No, this is what the prophet Joel said. He wrote that in these last days God said that He would pour out His Holy Spirit on the people. Great wonders will happen, and everyone who calls on the Name of the Lord shall be saved.

"You men of Israel, you listen to me: God has given wonderful signs through Jesus of Nazareth, as you all know. But in accordance with God's purpose He was taken by wicked men and put to death by being nailed to a cross. Now God has raised Him from the dead, as David wrote in the psalms the words of the Lord, 'I was always seeing the Lord before Me; since He is at my right hand, I shall not be shaken. My body also will rest in hope, because You will not leave Me in the grave, nor will You let Your Holy One see decay.'

"My brothers," Peter reasoned, "you know that David is dead and buried and his tomb is with us to this day, so he could not be writing about himself when he says that he would not stay in the tomb. He must be speaking of Christ Who has died and is now alive again. And we have all seen Him. This Jesus Whom you crucified, God has now made Lord of all, as David says in another psalm."

When Peter had finished preaching the people were cut to the heart, and said, "If this has happened, what shall we do?"

Peter responded directly. "Repent and be baptized, every one of you, in the Name of Jesus Christ, so that your sins may be forgiven you."

Hundreds of people came to hear Peter as he warned them and pleaded with them to repent of their sins.

That day, about three thousand people who listened to Peter and the other disciples were convinced by the preaching, found peace in believing, and were baptized.

Every day they listened to the teaching of the apostles, they broke bread together, and spent their time in prayer. They were all filled with reverence and godly fear, and many signs and wonders were done by the apostles.

The believers visited one another's homes and those who were rich sold their possessions and shared their money with those who were poor.

They praised God together and every day more people were being added to the church.

The lame man

There was a poor man who could not walk, he was lame. He could not work, either. The only way he could obtain money was to sit outside the temple and beg people to give him something as they went into the temple. His friends carried him to the gate called Beautiful every day.

When Peter and John came up together to the temple to pray, the man asked them for a gift. Peter looked straight at him, so did John. Then Peter said: "Look at us!" The man thought they might give him something. But Peter said: "I have no silver or gold. But what I do have, I will give you. In the name of Jesus Christ of Nazareth, rise up and walk!" Then, taking his hand, he helped the crippled man to stand. Straightaway the man felt his feet and ankle bones become strong. He jumped up and began to walk about. Then, walking and jumping and praising God, he went into the temple with Peter and John.

All the people looked and saw that he was the man who always sat begging at the gate called Beautiful. They stood in astonishment and wonder at this miracle which had happened. People from all over the temple court came to see the man who that morning had been sitting begging at the gate.

This was a good opportunity for Peter to tell them of Jesus again.

"Men of Israel," he began, "Why are you so surprised? Why stare at us as if it were our own power or godliness which made this man walk? The God of our fathers, the God of Abraham, Isaac and Jacob, has glorified His servant Jesus. You handed Him over to Pilate, delivering Him to be killed, when Pilate wanted to release Him. You rejected the Holy and Righteous One and asked for a murderer to be released instead. You put to death the Prince of Life. Now God has raised Him from the dead, and we have seen and heard Him. He is not dead, but lives. It is by the name of Jesus and through His power that this man is now completely well in your presence.

"I know that you acted in ignorance, just as your rulers did. All has been fulfilled as the prophets said. Christ had to suffer for our sins.

"Repent, therefore, and turn to God, that your sins may be wiped away.

"Moses said, 'The Lord God will raise up a prophet like me and every soul that does not listen to Him will be destroyed from among the people.' All the prophets from Samuel onwards have said the same."

As they were speaking to the people, the priests and the captain of the temple guard, together with the Sadducees, came along. They were very angry that the apostles were teaching the people and proclaiming that Jesus was raised from the dead.

So they arrested Peter and John and put them in jail.

The next day the rulers and elders held a meeting. The High Priest was there, and all the important people. Peter and John were brought in before them. "Can you tell us how it is that this man can now walk? From where do you get your power to do this?"

Then Peter, filled with the Holy Spirit, answered them politely:

"Rulers and elders of the people, are we on trial today to say how this poor man was healed? Are you asking us how and why he was made to stand and walk? Let me clearly tell all of you here and all the people of Israel that it was done in the name of Jesus Christ of Nazareth: the One you crucified is the One whom God has raised from the dead. This man stands here today made quite well by His Name. You rejected Jesus, but there is no other name under Heaven by which we must be saved."

When they saw how confident and bold Peter and John were, and when they discovered that they were ordinary and uneducated men, they were astonished. Seeing the healed man standing there, they could say nothing. For this was a truly wonderful miracle.

So they conferred together. "What shall we do?" they asked. "We shall just have to warn them not to speak or teach in the name of Jesus any longer."

So they commanded Peter and John to say nothing more about Jesus.

"Tell us," they answered, "Do you think it right to listen to your orders, or to listen to God? We cannot possibly stop speaking about the marvellous things we have seen and heard."

"You had better do what we say," the rulers admonished, "or it will be the worse for you!"

But all the people glorified God for what had happened, for the man who had been healed was over forty years of age.

Peter and John were released; they returned to their friends, and reported to them all that the chief priests and elders had said. After this, they all prayed together and said:

"O Lord, it is You Who made everything; King David said in the psalms that the rulers stand up against the Lord and against His Christ, and that is what they are doing. Consider, O Lord, how they threaten us, and give us courage to speak Your word to the people, and stretch out Your hand to show signs and wonders to the people, by the name of Jesus."

When they had prayed the place where they were gathering shook, and they were all filled with the Holy Spirit and began to speak the word of God fearlessly.

Stephen is stoned

Wonderful things were happening in Jerusalem. Sick people were being healed, and more and more people were becoming believers in the Lord Jesus Christ. Several thousand people were baptized, and many priests also became obedient to the faith. Many were poor and in need, but such was the love of the believers for one another that those who had plenty sold their possessions, and brought the money to the apostles, who distributed it to those in need.

The apostles' main work was to pray and to teach the people, so they said, "We do not have enough time to do everything, you must choose other men to look after the money and give it out to the widows, the orphan children and others who cannot work. Choose seven good men, full of faith and of the Holy Spirit, and let them do this work so that the money will be given out fairly."

So they brought seven godly men to the apostles, who laid their hands on them and prayed for them. Then the work of God spread, and many more became disciples of Christ, including many of the priests. Now one of these men was named Stephen. God's blessing was on him in a special way; not only did he perform signs and miracles, but he was also a very good preacher.

Some of the Jews were upset at what he taught about Jesus, and began to dispute with him. But they could not answer his arguments, nor meet the wisdom and conviction with which he spoke. They were determined to stop him teaching the things they did not like the people to hear, so they stirred up the people, the elders and the scribes. They also persuaded people to say that Stephen spoke against God and what the scriptures taught.

As a result, Stephen was hauled before the council of the chief priests. Then dishonest people were brought along and said, "He is always preaching against the law of God and against our temple. He ought to be stoned to death." As the men in the council looked at him, they saw that his face shone like an angel.

"Is this true?" the High Priest asked. Then Stephen answered the question by giving them a sermon explaining what God had done with their nation over many years. This is what he said:

"Hear me, brothers and fathers in Israel," he began. Then he reminded them of how their nation had begun with Abraham, and God's promises to him. He related how Abraham had obeyed God and had come to the land in which they were now living. Stephen reminded them of Isaac and Jacob and his twelve sons who became heads of the twelve tribes of Israel; he related the story of Joseph, telling them of how he was sold into Egypt. "But God was good to him," Stephen continued, "and delivered him out of all his troubles, and he became ruler over all the land. When the famine came and there was no food in Canaan, our father Jacob sent his sons to buy food in Egypt, so that they would not starve. On their second visit, Joseph told his brothers who he was, and sent for his father and all the family to be with him. Jacob and his brothers and all their children came and were kept alive.

"You remember," Stephen went on, "that in Egypt our people increased in numbers and we became a nation there. After many years a new king came to the throne and ill-treated our people, made us slaves and killed our little ones, but Moses was saved and brought up by Pharaoh's daughter in the king's palace. There he became a mighty prince. But you know how he had to escape from Egypt when he killed that Egyptian who was beating a Jewish slave.

"For many years Moses was a shepherd in the land of Midian, until God spoke to him out of the bush that burned and sent him back to Egypt to deliver His people from their slavery, and lead them to the Promised Land."

He went on to tell them how Moses had given them God's laws which they had not obeyed. Stephen also told them of the tent of worship Moses commanded to be made and how later on Solomon had built the temple for God.

Up to that point, the Council could say nothing against Stephen. They knew that all this was true from the Holy Scripture. Stephen was not speaking against the law of God, nor against the temple of the Lord. They also knew that their forefathers had rebelled against God and His prophets.

But now, Stephen annoyed them by recalling Solomon's prayer in which he said: "Heaven cannot contain You, Lord. How much less can this house which I have built." And, from the prophet Isaiah, Stephen quoted: "Where is the house you could build Me?" Stephen was really saying, "This temple cannot contain God, He is too big; but He will dwell with those who have a humble heart and obey His word."

"Our people have not obeyed God's laws," Stephen went on. "They persecuted the prophets who told them of the coming of the Righteous One, and now you are doing the very same. You have killed the Christ and want to destroy His followers. You are just like those who killed God's prophets!"

When they heard this, the chief priests were furious with Stephen. They did not like his telling them that they had killed the Messiah Who had been sent to them. In a rage they ground their teeth. But Stephen, full of the Holy Spirit, and looking up to Heaven, saw the glory of God, and Jesus standing at God's right hand.

"Look!" said he, "I see the heavens open, and the Son of Man standing at the right hand of God." The chief priests began to shout and put their hands to their ears. They would not listen to what Stephen was saying. They rushed him out of the court and began to pick up stones to stone him. As he was struck he kneeled down and cried out with a loud voice: "Lord, do not charge them with this sin!" It was the last thing he said. For there his life was ended by the cruel stones.

Those people who were casting the stones had thrown off their outer clothes and given them to a young man to look after. His name was Saul. He came from Tarsus, and had been trained by the best teacher in Jerusalem to become a Pharisee. Saul was very proud of the Jewish faith, and he wanted to see this man Stephen stoned to death.

When it was all over, the Christians mourned for Stephen, and godly men took his body away to be buried.

This was the beginning of great trouble for the followers of Jesus. The rulers commanded that any disciples of Jesus should be punished. They went into their homes and dragged them off to prison. Saul was determined to destroy the church, stop the people from meeting together, and prevent this gospel from spreading to others.

As a result, the people began to leave Jerusalem and escape to Judaea and Samaria. Wherever they went, they spread the news of the Christian faith with the result that people in other parts also came to believe in Jesus. Many more miracles happened which showed that God was with the believers, and there was great joy among all those who came to trust in Christ.

Saul! Saul!

The Christians who were driven out of Jerusalem spread the good news of Jesus wherever they went. Saul went after them. The High Priest gave him letters which allowed him to go and arrest the followers of Jesus and have them chained up in prison. Saul wanted to stamp out this new religion wherever it appeared.

He was on the way north with his guards to go to the city of Damascus intending to bring back to Jerusalem as many believers as he could. Just as he was approaching the city a bright light from Heaven suddenly shone all around him, and he was dazzled. He fell to the ground and heard a voice saying:

"Saul, Saul, why are you persecuting Me?"

In great surprise he asked, "Who are You, Lord?" The voice said, "I am Jesus. You are persecuting Me."

Trembling with astonishment, Saul asked: "Lord, what do You want me to do?"

Jesus answered, "Now get up and go into the city. There you will be told what to do."

The men travelling with him were speechless. They also had heard the voice, but had seen no one.

Saul got up, but he could not see. So they led him by the hand into Damascus. For three days Saul was without his sight, and for three days he neither ate nor drank anything, while he wondered and prayed about what had happened to him, and thought about the Lord Jesus Who had spoken to him.

Now there was a disciple in Damascus called Ananias. The Lord came to him in a vision: "Ananias." He replied, "Yes, Lord?"

"Go to the house of Judas in the street called Straight, and ask for Saul of Tarsus. He is praying there. He has seen a vision of a man called Ananias coming and laying his hands on him to bring back his sight."

"But, Lord," Ananias answered, "I have heard from many people how much harm this man has done to Your saints in Jerusalem, and he has come here to take away anyone who calls on Your name."

The Lord said to Ananias, "Go and do as I say. I have chosen him to be My servant. I am going to send him to other lands, as well as to the Jews. He will tell them about Me, and I have to show him how much he is to suffer for My name."

So Ananias went and found Saul. And when he had found him he laid his hands on him and said these good words. "Brother Saul, the Lord Jesus, Who appeared to you on the road as you came, has sent me, so that you may receive your sight and be filled with the Holy Spirit."

Immediately, Saul was able to see. He was then baptized; and had something to eat.

Saul was now to be known as Paul. He stayed in Damascus, made friends with the other disciples there, and began to preach in the Jewish synagogues that Jesus is the Son of God.

Everyone was amazed at the change. "This is the man," they said, "who came to arrest the Christians and take them as prisoners to the chief priests. But now listen to him preaching that Jesus is the Christ!"

The Jews were angry that Saul the persecutor had now become Paul the Christian. They made a conspiracy to kill him, but the disciples came to hear of it, and they arranged for Paul to escape. After the city gates were closed they let him down the wall of the city in a basket. So Paul made his way back to Jerusalem.

There the disciples were afraid of him. They could not believe that he had become a Christian; they thought it was a trick to catch them, so they kept away from him.

But Barnabas went to him, and brought him to the apostles. Paul told them how he had seen the Lord on the road, and what Jesus had told him. He then spoke boldly in the name of the Lord in Jerusalem. Some of the Jews began arguing with Paul and became so angry with him that they tried to kill him. So some disciples went away with Paul to Caesarea, and then to Tarsus.

After this, the churches throughout Judaea, Samaria and Galilee had peace. The believers increased more and more, and they learned how to live in the fear of the Lord and in the comfort of the Holy Spirit.

Peter's travels

The apostle Peter travelled through all parts of the country visiting the churches in every place.

When he came to Lydda he found a man named Aeneas who had been bedridden for eight years. Peter said to him: "Aeneas, Jesus Christ makes you well. Get up and make your bed," – which he did immediately! This caused many people to turn to the Lord in that region.

In Joppa the disciples were very sad because of the death of a lady called Dorcas. Her other name was Tabitha. She had been a very kind and busy person, one who had spent her life helping other people. As the disciples had heard that Peter was not far away in Joppa they sent two men there asking him to come to Joppa quickly. When Peter arrived the poor people began showing him the clothes that Dorcas had made for them. With tears in their eyes they showed him to an upstairs room where her body was laid. Peter sent everyone out of the room, then knelt down and prayed. After that he turned to the body and said, "Tabitha, arise!" She opened her eyes, and when she saw Peter she sat up. Then he took her by her hand, and she stood up. Peter called to her friends to come into the room where to their surprise and great happiness they found their Dorcas alive and well. When the people in Joppa heard about this great miracle, many more believed in the Lord Jesus.

Peter stayed with the Christians in Joppa for some time and lodged with a man called Simon the tanner.

About thirty miles up the coast from Joppa was the town of Caesarea, and stationed there was a centurion in the Roman army of occupation. He was a good, devout and God-fearing man. He gave generously to those in need, and he prayed regularly every day. One afternoon, at about three o'clock, he saw a vision from God. An angel came to him and said: "Cornelius!"

Cornelius was surprised and stared at the angel in fear. "What do you want, Lord?" he asked.

"Your prayers and your gifts to the poor have come up before God as a sacrifice to be remembered. Now send men to Joppa to bring a man by the name of Peter who is staying with Simon the tanner, whose house is by the seaside. He has something to tell you."

When the angel had gone, Cornelius called two of his servants and a soldier who was a very devout man and was always with him, and told them all that had happened. The next day he sent them on their journey to Joppa. About midday, as they were approaching the city, Peter went up to the roof-top of the house to pray. He was very hungry, and while he was there he too saw a vision. He saw Heaven and a great sheet coming down full of all kinds of animals, birds and creeping things. A voice said, "Rise, Peter, kill and eat!"

Peter replied, "No, no, Lord, I have never eaten anything which our law says is unclean, however hungry I am." The vision came again, and again the voice said, "Rise, Peter, kill and eat. What God has cleansed, do not call unclean." This happened three times, after which the sheet on which the creatures were lowered was taken up into Heaven.

Peter was trying to understand what the vision meant when the men from Joppa came to the door. The Spirit of God said to Peter, "There are men looking for you. Go down and see them. I have sent them to you. Do not be afraid to go with them."

So Peter invited them into the house, and they told him that their master had seen a vision in which he was told to send for Peter. They told him, "Our master is a Roman centurion, but he fears God and is respected by the people of your nation."

Now Peter would not have considered it right for a Jew to go into the house of a Gentile soldier, but his dream had told him three times that he must not call other people unholy or unclean, so the next day he made the trip from Joppa to Caesarea with the men who had been sent to bring him. Cornelius was waiting for them, and as soon as Peter came into the house, Cornelius met him, fell down at his feet, and worshipped him. But Peter raised him up. "I am only a man," he said. "You must not worship me."

Cornelius had brought in a good company of people.

Then Peter said, "You know that it is not considered right for a Jew to associate with foreigners, but God has shown me in a vision that I am not to call anyone unholy or unclean. So I have come. Now, why have you sent for me?"

Then Cornelius told him of the angel and what he had said. "So I sent for you immediately," said Cornelius. "Now we are all here before God to hear what you have been commanded to tell us from the Lord."

Peter began: "I understand now," he said, "that Gentiles, people from among other nations besides the Jews, are acceptable to God, and I must not call other people unclean.

"You will have heard about Jesus of Nazareth and what He did and taught throughout Galilee and Judaea; how God anointed Him with the Holy Spirit and with power, and how He went about doing good and healing all who were oppressed and unwell. We were with Him and saw all these things. We also saw Him put to death on the cross. But God raised Him up on the third day, and we and many others saw Him again. We ate and drank with Him after they had killed Him. We have been commanded to preach to all, and to tell everyone that Jesus is the One appointed by God to be the Judge of those who live, as well as those who have died. All the prophets have written about Him, saying that everyone who believes in Him will receive forgiveness of sins."

While Peter was still speaking, the Holy Spirit fell on all those who were listening to him.

The Jews who came with Peter were astonished as they saw the Holy Spirit coming upon these Gentiles as He had done on the Jews before.

"Surely," Peter exclaimed, "we cannot refuse to baptize those who have received the Holy Spirit just as we did!"

So they were baptized in the name of Jesus. Then Peter stayed with them for a few days.

The Christians in Judaea and Jerusalem heard that Peter had gone into the house of a Gentile and had preached to Gentiles and baptized them. When Peter went back to Jerusalem they said to him, "We hear that you have entered the house of a Gentile and have eaten with Gentile people! As a good Jew, you should not do that!"

So Peter explained to them exactly what had happened. He told them about the vision and how the Holy Spirit had directed him to go to the house of Cornelius.

When they heard what Peter had to say they no longer objected to what he had done. They said, "So the Lord also receives Gentiles who repent of their sins and believe in Him!" Then they glorified God Who accepts Gentiles into His everlasting kingdom as well as Jews.

The first missionaries

As the Christians travelled to other parts they told people in those places about the wonderful things which had happened. They spoke of the coming of Jesus and what He had said and done. They told of the death that He died and how He was raised from the dead and was seen and heard again. The Holy Spirit was with the Christians and the love they had for one another made a great impression on all who saw them. A great number of people believed and then turned to the Lord. When the church in Jerusalem heard this they sent Barnabas as far as Antioch in Syria where they were to teach and encourage the Christians there.

Barnabas was a man full of faith and of the Holy Spirit, and a great many people were added to the church there. But Barnabas needed some more help to teach all the people in the church the way of God. So he went to Tarsus to fetch his friend Paul. They then spent a whole year in Antioch teaching those who had turned to the Lord. It was here in Antioch that believers in Christ were first called Christians.

As the people in the church were praying and fasting, the Holy Spirit impressed upon them that they should send Paul and Barnabas out to other regions to preach the gospel. So they laid their hands on them, and sent them off to preach the gospel in other parts. Taking John Mark with them they went down to Seleucia and sailed from there to the island of Cyprus, where they proclaimed the word of God in the synagogues of the Jews.

The governor of the island asked Paul and Barnabas to come and tell him their message, but a false prophet who deceived the people tried to turn the governor away from the Christian faith.

Paul, full of the Holy Spirit, looked steadily at him and said, "O you, full of deceit and fraud, you are a son of the devil! Will you not stop turning people away from the true God? The hand of the Lord is upon you and you shall be blind for a time."

Immediately, all was dark for him and he called for someone to lead him by the hand.

THE MISSIONARY JOURNEYS OF THE APOSTLE PAUL

First Journey
Second Journey
Third Journey
Fourth Journey

MACEDONIA

Rome
Three Taverns
Forum of Appius

Adriatic Sea

Philippi
Thessalonica

ITALY

Berea

Puteoli

Pompeii

Rhegium

SICILY

Corinth

Cenchraea

Syracuse

ACHAIA

MALTA

THRACIA

BITHINIA

GALATIA

MYSIA

Troas

Pergamos

Sardis

Smyrna

Philadelphia

Ephesus

Laocidea

Colosse

Miletus

Cnidus

Rhodes

Patara

CRETE

Fair Havens

Aegean Sea

ens

CAPPADOCIA

Antioch

Iconium

Lystra

Derbe

Tarsus

PISIDIA

Perga

Attalia

LYCAONIA

CILICIA

LICIA

Myra

Seleucia

Salamis

CYPRUS

Paphos

Sidon

Tyre

Caesarea

Jerusalem

Alexandria

Then the governor believed, having understood the teaching of the Lord, and being astonished at what was done.

From there Paul and Barnabas took ship to the mainland and came to Perga and Antioch in Pisidia. There they entered the synagogue. After the Law and the Prophets had been read, the rulers said to Paul and Barnabas, "If you have anything to say to us explaining the scripture, be free to speak."

So Paul stood up and began: "You men of Israel, and you who fear God, I do have something to tell you." Then he showed them from their Old Testament scriptures that God had promised that a Saviour would come from the family of King David. He then told them about Jesus and what had been done to Him in Jerusalem, and how God had raised Him from the dead.

"It is through Jesus Christ that forgiveness of sins is given, and it is for everyone who believes," he said.

But the Jews did not like the apostles to be teaching the Gentiles. Paul told them, "If you will not listen to what we have to say and do not want everlasting life, then we turn to the Gentiles to tell them." So the Gospel was spread all around that region, but the Jews harassed Paul and Barnabas and finally drove them out of the locality.

They went off to other cities – Lystra and Derbe in Lycaonia, and the surrounding region. A man who could not use his legs since he was born was made well and able to walk, and many came to believe in the Lord Jesus. But the Jews again tried to turn the people away from the message of the apostles. Some of the Jews from Antioch and Iconium came and stoned Paul. They dragged him out of the city, supposing him to be dead. But while the disciples stood around him he got up and then went back into the city.

Next day, Barnabas and Paul moved on to other places, encouraging the Christians and appointing elders in every church.

Then they returned to the church which had sent them out on that first missionary journey. They reported to them all the things that God had done in opening the door of faith to Gentile people.

More missionary journeys

The apostle Paul kept thinking about the people in the churches that had been formed. He wanted to see them again and to help them on in their Christian life. He also had a great desire to go beyond these countries to other lands where the people had not yet heard about Jesus. This time he went with a man named Silas, and was glad to see again the believers in Derbe, Lystra and Iconium, and the other Christians in the region of Galatia and Mysia.

At Troas, Paul had a vision in the night of a man calling him to go across the sea to Macedonia. "Come over to Macedonia and help us!" he called. So Paul and Silas took ship and went to Europe. One of the cities they came to was called Philippi. On the Sabbath Day they went outside the city to the river to pray. There they met Lydia, a woman who owned a business selling purple materials. As she listened to Paul's message of Jesus the Saviour, the Lord opened her heart to Him. She was baptized together with all the members of her household. "If you believe me to be a faithful Christian," she said, "come to my house to stay while you are here."

Other things happened in Philippi. A slave girl who was possessed by an evil spirit began following Paul and his friends around. She kept crying out: "These men are the servants of the Most High God; they are telling us the way of salvation!" This she did every day. At last, Paul turned around and said to the spirit in her: "I command you in the name of Jesus Christ to come out of her!" And he came out of her that very hour.

Now, the masters of this slave girl used to make a great deal of money by using her to tell people their fortunes through the evil spirit. Her masters were angry now that she could do this no longer. They seized Paul and Silas and dragged them to court. All those who did not like the preaching of Paul and Silas came and shouted for them to be beaten with rods. So the magistrates had them flogged and thrown into prison.

The jailer was commanded to keep them safely. He put them in an inner cell and fastened their feet with chains. That night they could not go to sleep. Although their backs were bleeding and they were in much pain, Paul and Silas began to pray and to sing hymns to the Lord. The other prisoners had never heard anything like this before. Suddenly, there was an earthquake. The ground shook violently, the doors were loosed, and everyone's chains came away from the wall. The jailer woke up with a start, and when he saw the prison doors open he thought that all his prisoners had escaped. He would have to die for not keeping them safely. He drew his sword to kill himself.

"Don't harm yourself!" Paul shouted. "We are all here!"

The jailer knew that it was the God of Paul and Silas Who was looking after His own. He was afraid, and falling down before them, he cried, "Sirs, what must I do to be saved?"

They said, "Believe on the Lord Jesus Christ and you will be saved, and all in your house."

Then they explained the way of Christ to all the family, who believed their words and were baptized. The jailer washed their wounds for them, and gave them a meal.

In the morning the magistrates gave orders that Paul and Silas were to be released. "You may go in peace," they said. But Paul made them come and apologize first for what they had done. Then Paul and Silas went back to Lydia's house.

From there they travelled to Thessalonica where Paul preached in the Jews' synagogue on three Sabbath days. He showed them from their own Old Testament scriptures that Christ was to suffer and then rise again from the dead, proving to them that Jesus Christ was truly the Messiah. Some of the Jews believed what he preached and joined Paul and Silas, as did many of the God-fearing Greeks and a number of the leading women in the city. But most of the Jews did not like what they were hearing and incited some bad characters from the market place to start a riot. They attacked the home of Jason where Paul and Silas were staying, but they could not find the apostles. So they dragged Jason and some other believers to the court and stirred up the crowd against them. But the rulers let them go, while the friends of Paul and Silas sent them away that night to Berea.

Here they went to the Jewish synagogue as they usually did. The Jews there gave Paul and Silas a fair hearing, listening carefully to what the apostles had to say. Then they searched in their scriptures to see if the things that were preached were true. As a result, many of the Jews became Christians, including many of the leading men and women in the city.

But when the Jews at Thessalonica heard that God's word was being preached in Berea they came there and stirred up more trouble for the messengers of the Lord. So Paul left to go and preach the gospel in other places, leaving Silas and his young friend Timothy to follow him later on.

Athens was the next stop. Paul was distressed when he saw all the idols which were worshipped in that city. The learned men and scholars there wanted to hear what Paul had to say. When he told them that God required them to repent of their sins, they told him that they would hear him another day. A few believed the word he preached. But some laughed at him when he spoke about Jesus having been raised from the dead.

Corinth in Greece was the furthest place Paul and Silas reached before they turned back to call again on the churches on their long journey home. Every Sabbath Day Paul reasoned with the Jews in the synagogue at Corinth. In this city, Paul made tents in order to get money to meet his travelling expenses, and it was there that he met two Christians whose work was also to make tents.

Paul came back by boat across the Mediterranean Sea, calling at Ephesus on the way. Many people came to Ephesus to worship at the temple of a goddess called Diana. They did not want to know about Jesus the Christ, and there was a great disturbance and commotion in the town when Paul had first visited Ephesus. He and his friends were in danger of being mobbed. But a church was formed there composed of people who became very fine Christians. Paul loved them, as he did all the Christians. The last time he saw the elders of the church there he reminded them of how he had taught them, cared for them, and instructed them. Then he told them that he would not be seeing them any more. The last thing he said to them was: "I showed you how to work hard so that you can help others. Remember the words of the Lord Jesus: 'It is more blessed to give than to receive.'"

When he had finished saying all these things they all knelt down and prayed and began to cry. As he departed they hugged and kissed him because he had been such a bringer of good news to them and had done so much good for them.

So they returned to the church at Jerusalem and Antioch.

Trouble in Jerusalem

The apostle Paul made four missionary journeys. He was away from his homeland for a long time. There were many dangers and trials which he had to endure. In some places he was beaten, at other times he was put in prison; sometimes he was mobbed by the crowd, or stoned. At times he was cold and hungry; at other times, hot and thirsty. Five times he was lashed with thirty-nine strokes of the whip. Three times he was shipwrecked. He was in danger from robbers, and attacked by Jews, as well as by Gentiles. There were dangers in the city and dangers in the wilderness. He endured many hardships, including nights without sleep. In addition to all this, he was concerned that the Christians should know what God wanted, and be living good lives for God everywhere. He was worried about teachers who came to the churches and taught the people the wrong things.

From prison and from other places Paul wrote letters to the churches. In them he explained the wonders of the Christian faith. He instructed the Christians how they should live, and how to run their churches, and he told them about things that were to come, including resurrection day, judgment day and, at the end of the world, the return of the Lord Jesus Who will come in glory for His own people, as He promised.

There were many Jews who did not like Paul travelling around teaching the way Jesus had. Paul was back again in Jerusalem. There he told the church what great things God had done in forming so many churches of people who had come to love and serve Jesus the Lord. But many of the Jews were angry that he should have told all those Jews, as well as Gentiles in other parts, about Jesus.

Paul went along to the temple where he was recognized by Jews who knew him. They dragged him out, and people from all over the city came together shouting and making a great noise. Roman soldiers were sent to see what the trouble was, and they rescued Paul. The commander wanted to know what he had done wrong. Paul said, "I am a Jew. Let me talk to the people in their own Hebrew language." Then they all listened as he told them how he had been converted on the way to Damascus, and had seen the Lord Jesus. After a while they would listen to him no longer. "He ought to die!" they shouted.

The following night, in prison, the Lord Himself stood by Paul and said to him: "Take courage, Paul. You have witnessed well for Me in Jerusalem. Now you will go and witness for Me in Rome."

Forty Jews made a plot to kill Paul, but the commander sent him with two hundred soldiers to Caesarea by night. There Paul was kept in prison for two years, although he was innocent. As a Roman citizen, as well as a Jew, Paul demanded to be sent to Rome to be tried. So it was decided to send him by boat with soldiers and other prisoners to Rome.

Shipwrecked!

The soldiers and their prisoners were put aboard a ship which was to sail along the coast of Asia toward Rome. The wind was blowing against them. So they had to leave the coast and sail south toward the island of Crete. The journey had taken many days. The winter storms would now be expected. Paul advised them to shelter by the island, but the captain of the ship and the commander of the soldiers decided to go on to a better shelter. A gentle southerly breeze was blowing which they thought would take them along on their course.

But before very long the wind blew violently, driving them out to sea. The timbers began to creak as the ship was tossed up and down on the fearsome waves. The wind screamed through the rigging as the boat was swamped by the seas. After three terrible days they began to throw the cargo and the ship's tackle overboard to lighten the ship. Their sails torn, they had no idea where they were.

After many days on that raging sea, Paul stood up and said to them, "You should have listened to my advice and then you would not have had all this loss and damage. Now take courage, for no one will drown, but the ship will be lost. This I know, because the angel of the Lord stood beside me in the night. 'Do not be afraid, Paul,' he said, 'you must stand before Caesar. All those who sail with you will also be saved.' Therefore take heart, for I believe God."

The storm lasted two whole weeks, and the seas were still boisterous when, about midnight, the sailors on watch believed that they were near some land. Taking soundings with their line, they found there was 120 feet of water below them, then 90 feet. They knew that they would soon be driven on to the rocks, so four anchors were cast out to hold the boat until the morning.

In the morning Paul said, "You have not had a proper meal for days. If you want to survive, get yourself some food." Then he gave thanks to God and they all had something to eat. There were 276 persons on the ship and when they had eaten enough, the crew let go the anchors, hoisted a sail and ran toward the shore. The bows stuck fast; then great waves crashed on the boat, breaking it up. The

centurion commanded those who could swim to jump overboard. The rest, holding on to pieces of the ship, were washed ashore.

They discovered that the island on which they had landed was Malta. The natives were kind and welcomed them to their island. They lit a fire, for the survivors were cold and wet. As Paul helped to collect wood for the fire, a poisonous snake bit him and held on to his hand, but he managed to shake it off into the fire. The people expected Paul to swell up, or suddenly fall down dead, but nothing at all happened to him. Later on, they asked him to come and see an older man who was very ill. Paul went along, prayed and laid his hands on the man, and he was healed.

Others who were suffering from various diseases were brought to Paul and they were healed also. So the people of the island looked after those who had been shipwrecked.

After three months they were able to board a ship for Syracuse in Sicily, which then sailed on up the coast of Italy to Puteoli where Paul found some Christians with whom he was able to stay until arrangements were made to travel to Rome. The apostle was greatly cheered because some believers in Rome who had heard that he was on the way came out to meet him.

In Rome he was kept under guard, but Paul sent messages to the Jews to come and see him. When they came he explained why he was there. They said, "We would like to hear about the Christian faith because some people speak against it. Tell us all about it."

Paul was allowed to rent a house in which he stayed. The Jews came to hear him explain to them that it was in fulfilment of the law of Moses and the writings of the prophets that Jesus the Messiah had come, as God had promised, to take away the sins of His people.

Some believed what Paul had told them. Others did not. So Paul said to them, "The prophet of old wrote, saying that you would not understand. Therefore, I turn now to tell the Gentiles that the salvation of God is for them."

For two years Paul was kept under guard in the house, and every day people came and he was allowed to speak to them of all the things concerning the kingdom of God and Jesus the Christ.

That is the story of how the good news of God began to be spread throughout the world – the world that God loved so much that He gave His only begotten Son, that whoever believes in Him should not perish but have everlasting life.

That good news is still spreading around the world. How happy are the people whose trust is in the Lord, and in His Son Jesus Christ.

The happy ending

The apostle Paul, as well as Peter, James and John, could not be with the churches which had been formed, all the time. They wrote letters to them explaining the purposes of God for His people in the church. We call these letters epistles, and they are to be found in our Bible today.

The last book in the Bible is the most amazing of all. It is full of strange visions which all have wonderful meanings. There are letters from the Lord Jesus to the churches. There are visions of Jesus in Heaven with everyone worshipping Him. There are descriptions of the enemy of God and the great war between him and his followers, and Jesus and His followers. The wicked one and all who belong to him are judged and punished, and they are banished from the presence of God for ever.

At the end, we find that there is a wonderful place prepared for all those who love and obey our Lord Jesus and belong to Him. Here there will never be any more pain or trouble, sadness or sickness. It will be a place where God's servants will always be able to serve Him happily. Jesus and His people will be happily married for ever.

The words of the Lord Jesus on the last page are: "Surely, I am coming quickly." And those who love Him, answer: "Amen, come, Lord Jesus."

Index of Stories and Bible references

THE OLD TESTAMENT

In the beginning (Genesis 1 & 2) — 10
In the beautiful garden (Genesis 2 & 3) — 13
Cain and Abel (Genesis 4) — 16
The flood (Genesis 6–9) — 19
The tower of Babel (Genesis 11) — 24
God calls Abram (Genesis 12–21) — 26
    Abram leaves his home — 26
    Abram and Lot — 26
    God's promise — 27
    Lot escapes — 30
    Isaac is born — 30
Where is the lamb? (Genesis 22) — 31
The twins (Genesis 24–33) — 34
Joseph is sold (Genesis 37–40) — 42
Pharaoh's dreams (Genesis 41) — 46
Joseph's brothers (Genesis 42–45) — 49
Jacob goes to Egypt (Genesis 46–50) — 55
Moses is born (Exodus 1 & 2) — 56
Moses escapes to Midian (Exodus 2) — 59
The bush that did not burn (Exodus 3 & 4) — 60
"Let My people go!" (Exodus 5–10) — 63
The Exodus (Exodus 11–15) — 67
Living in the wilderness (Exodus 15–17) — 70
They camp by the mountain (Exodus 17–19) — 73
    Attacked by the Amalekites — 73
    Wise advice — 73
    God speaks — 74
The commands of God (Exodus 20–32) — 75
The last days of Moses (Exodus 33–40) — 78
    (Deuteronomy 31–34)
Crossing the river (Joshua 1–5) — 80
Jericho falls (Joshua 6) — 82
What happened at Ai and Gibeon (Joshua 7 & 8) — 86
The Judges (Joshua 24) — 89
    (Judges 1–5)

Gideon (Judges 6 & 7) — 90
Samson (Judges 13–16) — 92
Ruth and Naomi (Ruth 1–4) — 97
The story of Hannah (I Samuel 1–7) — 100
A king for Israel (I Samuel 8–16) — 102
David and Goliath (I Samuel 17) — 105
Saul is jealous (I Samuel 18–31) — 108
    (II Samuel 1)
King David becomes great and sins (II Samuel 6, 7, 11) — 111
Nathan talks to David (II Samuel 12) — 113
Absalom tries to be king (II Samuel 13–18) — 117
Solomon becomes king (I Kings 1–11) — 120
Elijah and the wicked king (I Kings 11, 12, 17, 18, 21, 22) — 123
Elisha follows Elijah (I Kings 19) — 127
    (II Kings 2, 5)
    Naaman — 129
Amos, the shepherd preacher (Amos) — 130
Isaiah and the army of Syria (II Kings 18, 19) — 132
    (II Chronicles 32)
    (Isaiah 6)
Good kings and bad (II Kings 21–23) — 135
    (II Chronicles 33–35)
Jeremiah, the sad prophet (Jeremiah 13, 18, 19, 24, 32, 37, 39, 40) — 138
Ezekiel's visions (Ezekiel 1–4, 47, 48) — 142
Daniel and the king's dream (Daniel 1, 2) — 143
The burning fiery furnace (Daniel 3) — 145
The den of lions (Daniel 4–6) — 148
Going home (Ezra 1, 2, 6, 7) — 152
    (Nehemiah 1, 2, 7, 12, 13)

THE NEW TESTAMENT

God's kingdom is coming 159

Angels appear (Luke 1) 160

How Jesus came (Luke 2) 163

Wise men arrive (Matthew 2) 168

Jesus goes to the temple (Luke 2) 170

Jesus is baptized (Matthew 3, 4) 174
(Mark 1)
(Luke 3, 4)

The first miracle (John 2) 177

Jesus visits Jerusalem (John 2, 3, 4) 181

Jesus returns to Galilee (John, 4, 5) 184
(Matthew 4, 5, 6, 7)
(Luke 5)
(Mark 3)

Two stories from the farm (Matthew 13) 190
The parable of the sower 190
The good seed 191

Miracles 192
The sick servant (Matthew 8) 192
The man at the pool (John 5) 192
The man who died – then lived (Luke 7) 194
The terrible storm (Luke 8) 194
A worried father and a woman of faith 195
(Matthew 9)

The good news spreads (Matthew 9, 10, 14) 196
(Luke 10)

Walking on the water (Mark 6) 199
(Matthew 14)

Who is Jesus? (Matthew 16, 17, 18) 201
(Mark 9, 10)

Jesus returns to Jerusalem (Luke 10, 12, 17) 205
(John, 11, 12)
The raising of Lazarus 206

The good shepherd (John 10) 210
(Luke 15)

A happy father (Luke 15) 212

The little man (Luke 19) 215

The wedding feast (Matthew 22, 25) 216

The King comes (Matthew 21, 24, 26) 218
(Mark 11, 12)
(Luke 19)
(John 12)

The last supper (Matthew 26) 222
(Mark 14)
(Luke 22)
(John 17)

Betrayed! (Matthew 26) 227
(Mark 14)
(Luke 22)
(John 14)

Crucified (Matthew 27) 229
(Mark 15)
(Luke 23)
(John 19)

He is risen! (Matthew 28) 232
(Mark 16)
(Luke 24)
(John 20 & 21)

The Holy Spirit comes (Acts 1 & 2) 239

The lame man (Acts 3) 242

Stephen is stoned (Acts 6 & 7) 245

Saul! Saul! (Acts 9) 249

Peter's travels (Acts 9, 10, 11) 252

The first missionaries (Acts 13 & 14) 255

More missionary journeys (Acts 15–20) 259

Trouble in Jerusalem (Acts 21–26) 262

Shipwrecked! (Acts 27 & 28) 264

The happy ending (The Revelation) 267